Simply Triangles

11 Deceptively Easy Quilts Featuring Stars, Daisies & Pinwheels

Barbara H. Cline

C&T PUBLISHING

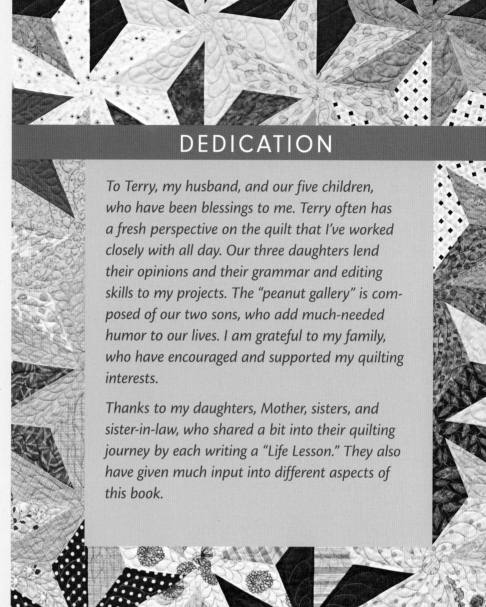

Text copyright © 2012 by Barbara H. Cline

Photography and Artwork copyright © 2012 by C&T Publishing, Inc.

Publisher: Amy Marson

Creative Director: Gailen Runge

Acquisitions Editor: Susanne Woods

Editor: Cynthia Bix

Technical Editors: Susan Nelsen and Joyce Lytle

Cover Designer: April Mostek

Book Designer: Christina D. Jarumay

Production Coordinator: Jenny Davis

Production Editors: Alice Mace Nakanishi and S. Michele Fry

Illustrator: Kirstie L. Pettersen

Photography by Christina Carty-Francis and Diane Pedersen of C&T Publishing, Inc., unless otherwise noted

Published by C&T Publishing, Inc., P.O. Box 1456, Lafayette, CA 94549

Library of Congress Cataloging-in-Publication Data

Cline, Barbara H.

Simply triangles : 11 deceptively easy quilts featuring stars, daisies & pinwheels / Barbara Cline.

p. cm.

ISBN 978-1-60705-421-4 (soft cover)

1. Patchwork--Patterns. 2. Quilting--Patterns. 3. Triangles--Miscellanea. I. Title.

TT835.C598 2011

746.46'041--dc23

2011019330

Printed in China

10 9 8 7 6 5

DEDICATION

To Terry, my husband, and our five children, who have been blessings to me. Terry often has a fresh perspective on the quilt that I've worked closely with all day. Our three daughters lend their opinions and their grammar and editing skills to my projects. The "peanut gallery" is composed of our two sons, who add much-needed humor to our lives. I am grateful to my family, who have encouraged and supported my quilting interests.

Thanks to my daughters, Mother, sisters, and sister-in-law, who shared a bit into their quilting journey by each writing a "Life Lesson." They also have given much input into different aspects of this book.

ACKNOWLEDGMENTS

Thanks to Ken and Phyllis Reeves, who own Patchwork Plus. They have given me many teaching opportunities to test my patterns in classes. They have also given me a flexible schedule.

It has been a delight to work with the staff members at C&T Publishing. Without their help, I could never have written this book. Their good ideas and expertise have been invaluable.

Another thanks to the generosity of fabric companies: P&B Textiles, RJR Fabrics, and Michael Miller Fabrics.

I also want to thank Joyce Horst for helping in writing "My Quilting Journey."

CONTENTS

Introduction

My Quilting Journey

I was brought up with six sisters and a brother in a loving Mennonite home in the beautiful Virginia countryside. My memories are rich with happy times spent frolicking along the banks of the North River and joining in the escapades of a rambunctious tribe. Of course, there were less delightful days when long rows of green beans needed to be picked and canned, and weeds hoed in seemingly endless rows of corn. But the rewards of our summer labor stored in the cellar—home-canned jars and well-filled freezers—assured us of abundant, delicious meals all winter.

Winter was also the time for sewing. Sewing has been a part of my life since I was a little girl. Mother used her talent to provide practical and beautiful garments for our family. Her sewing machine kept humming long after the girls' dresses were completed, turning out an assortment of lingerie, nightgowns, caps, coats, and mittens for the growing family. Both of my grandmothers, Mary Wenger and Vera Heatwole, found spare minutes with a needle and thread to create elaborate embroidered works of art, which graced the bureaus, tabletops, and beds in our homes.

Scrappy Stars, 41″ × 43″, made and machine quilted by Barbara Cline

Grandmother Vera introduced me to quilting when I was ten years old. It was during those early childhood days that the seeds of sewing were planted that would later yield a harvest of piecing, designing, and quilting. The world of fabric came alive for me when my parents purchased a fabric store in my preteen years. I enjoyed learning about different fabrics and color combinations as well as working with people. Some of the store employees were expert quilters, and this further piqued my interest in the craft.

My six sisters have been another source of inspiration; they have inspired me to join a quilt guild, enter quilt contests, publish patterns, and learn new techniques. We also get together once a year for a sewing retreat. As our little ones grew up they started to join us, and it has been a great opportunity for them to focus on sewing as well as on building relationships and interacting with their grandmother, aunts, and cousins. The retreat has become one of the highlights of my year. Throughout this book, you'll find Life Lessons—simple, inspiring stories from some of these important people in my life.

About This Book

The eleven quilts featured in this book all have triangles as components. The triangle components themselves are constructed in a variety of ways using smaller triangles, trapezoids, and other shapes. Here are a few examples of the triangle designs used in this book. However, there is no limit to the number of ways you can create designs within a triangle; see what you can come up with on your own!

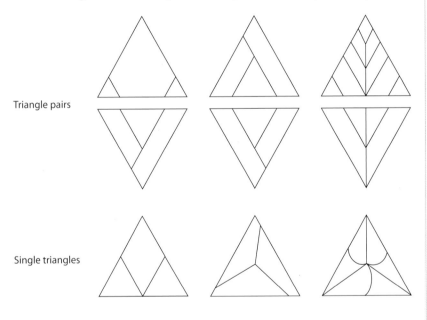

Triangle pairs

Single triangles

In some quilt designs, such as *Tumbling Stars* (page 26), the same triangle is repeated; in others, two different triangle designs are paired, as in *Fall Stars* (page 21).

The quilt projects in this book are presented in three sections. In Triangles to Stars (page 16), the triangles are put together to make star designs, beginning with simple one-piece triangles and moving on to more complex pieced triangles.

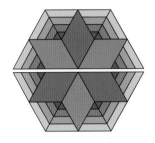

In Triangles to Daisies (page 53), triangles become daisies with the use of appliqué. Heart shapes that look like flower petals are appliquéd onto triangles, and six triangle points come together in the center to form a daisy.

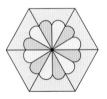

In the final section, Triangles to Pinwheels (page 65), triangles are almost magically transformed into jazzy pinwheel designs.

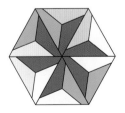

Triangle Quilt Basics

Supplies

A few simple techniques are used to create this wonderful variety of designs with triangles. Cutting techniques include cutting components with templates and cutting from strips, strip sets, and layers of fussy-cut fabric. Sewing techniques include appliquéing, sewing Y-seams, and using overlays.

In this chapter, you'll find information on the supplies and techniques you'll need to make the quilts in this book. All the quilts can be made using just basic quilting supplies. The following is a list of my favorites.

- **Rotary cutter,** with a sharp new blade

- **Rotary cutting mat,** 24″ × 36″

- **Rotary cutting rulers,** 6″ × 24″ and 4″ × 14″—The smaller ruler is not so clumsy and is easier to handle when cutting strips into triangles.

- **Creative Grids 60° Triangle** (8″ finished size) ruler—It is important to use this brand; others measure differently.

- **Pins**—I like the Nifty Notions Flower Head Pins. At 2″ long and .05mm thick, they are thin, long, and easy to pick up.

- **Sewing thread** to match fabric— You may need several different colors for each quilt.

- **¼″-wide presser foot** for your sewing machine—Check to make sure it is accurate.

- **Double-sided fusible web**—My choice is Shades SoftFuse; it leaves the projects soft.

- **Scissors** for clipping threads and trimming dog-ears

- **Seam ripper**

- **Template plastic**

- **Gluestick**

- **Iron and ironing board**

- **Spray starch**—I like Mary Ellen's Best Press because it doesn't have a lot of sizing. It doesn't make the fabric too stiff, but it does provide enough stability to keep the fabric from stretching.

- **Retayne** (G&K Craft Industries), *optional*—You can add this in your washing machine to keep fabrics from bleeding.

- **Perfect Piecer** (Jinny Beyer)—This tool has different angles to mark the ¼″ dots that are crucial for the pieces joined in a Y-seam.

- **Pen-style Chaco Liner** (Clover)— This marker is great for marking pattern pieces.

Fabric Preparation and Pressing

I prefer to preshrink my fabrics. Some fabrics shrink more than others. If you don't preshrink, they might shrink to different sizes after the quilt is pieced and washed, and the finished quilt may not lie flat. Also, I like to add Retayne to the washing machine when preshrinking to keep dark fabrics from bleeding.

As you cut template shapes and triangles, some of the edges will be cut on the bias. To keep these edges from stretching and distorting, handle the cut fabric pieces as little as possible and use spray starch to keep the fabric from stretching. Before cutting the fabric, spray it lightly with Best Press spray starch and press until dry.

In all the quilt instructions in this book, you will be told which way the seams should be pressed. Follow the pressing directions so that the seams will nest together. After each sewing step, I press without steam until I have sewn a completed block or triangle; then I use steam.

Cutting Shapes

The quilt designs in this book are based on triangles, either cut as whole triangle shapes or composed of different shapes—smaller triangles, trapezoids, and other four-sided shapes—combined in various ways. Before you cut the shapes, you will first cut a strip of fabric (or create a strip set), and from the strip, you will subcut individual shapes. You can use templates, with or without a rotary ruler, and the Creative Grids 60° Triangle ruler to cut the shapes. All the project templates are included in this book, but *some* of the pieces may be cut using the Creative Grids 60° Triangle. Because it's a time-saver, I prefer using this ruler whenever possible rather than templates. I've written the patterns so you can easily use the ruler in cutting some pieces for these projects.

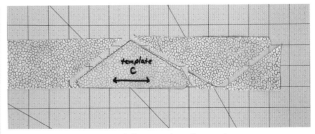

Keep grainline on edge of cut strip.

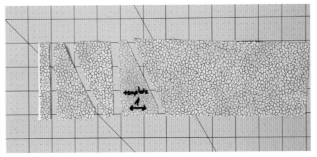

Never flip template unless told to; only rotate or slide.

CUTTING FROM STRIPS

Using templates

To make a template, photocopy the template pattern as directed in a particular project and roughly cut it out. Glue the paper cutout onto template plastic using a gluestick. Cut out the template on the pattern line, remove the paper, and label the template on the top side. Be sure to mark the grainline on the template as well.

Cutting template patterns from fabric strips is more efficient than cutting from whole pieces of fabric. It eliminates making little cuts in your fabric and requires fewer rotations of the template.

Place the fabric strip right side up and lay the template on the fabric strip near one end; cut around the template. The pattern will tell you how wide to cut the strip, and the template will show you where to position the grainline. Pictured is an example of how to position a template.

Note: When you cut the second shape, *rotate* or *slide* the template into the next position as shown; don't flip it unless the directions specifically tell you to flip.

Sometimes in a pattern there will be an "r" after a template letter, such as template Ar. This means you flip the A template over and then cut out the reverse shape. Then you proceed to rotate or slide this reversed template along the strip to cut the required number of pieces.

 tips

▪ If you tend to trim the plastic template when you cut the fabric, try laying a ruler against the template edge (not on top of the template); then remove the template and cut. Another option is to use a chalk pencil and draw around the template.

▪ I like to layer 4 strips of fabric on top of each other (keep all the right sides of the fabric facing up) and cut out 4 at a time. If you cut any more than this, you can distort the shape. Be sure to have a sharp blade in your rotary cutter. This helps keep the fabric from getting pushed forward and distorting the shape.

Using the Creative Grids 60°
Triangle ruler

Though all the templates are included for projects in this book, the Creative Grids ruler may be used to cut many triangles and trapezoids. Because using the ruler is easier and more precise than using templates, the project instructions throughout this book specifically indicate which pieces may be cut with this ruler.

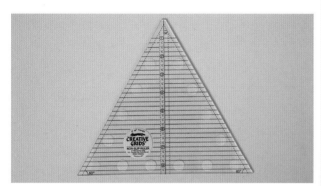

Creative Grids 60° Triangle (8″ finished size) ruler

60° TRIANGLES

 tip

This is an example of the project cutting instructions for 60° triangles:

Cut 2 strips 3¾″ x WOF; subcut into 14 triangles [3¾″], using template A.

The information in the brackets is the reference for the Creative Grids ruler. When using the ruler, disregard the template reference. These steps show how to use the ruler to cut these triangles [3¾″].

1. Cut a strip of fabric the width specified in the pattern directions by the width of the fabric (WOF) or as directed in the pattern. The photo example shows a 3¾″ strip.

2. Lay the triangle on top of the strip as shown and cut the desired triangle size. Cut along both sides of the triangle.

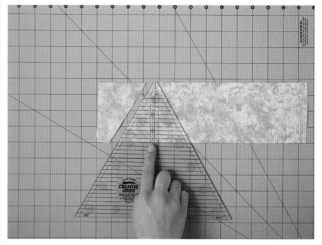

Bottom edge of fabric lines up with 3¾″ line on triangle.

3. Rotate the triangle ruler as shown. The 3¾″ line is now at the top edge of the fabric strip. Cut along the edge of the ruler to cut the next triangle. Continue to the end of the strip.

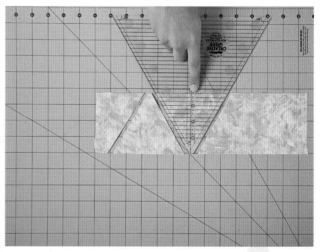

Rotate triangle.

30° TRIANGLES

1. Cut a strip of fabric the width specified in the pattern directions, and fold it in half lengthwise. The photo example shows a folded 4½" strip with the fold to the right. Make a straight cut on the left end of the strip.

2. Place the ruler on the fabric strip, lining up the top of the ruler with the top edge of the strip. The bottom edge of the fabric should be even with the 4½" mark on the ruler. Line up the cut fabric edges with the *left* vertical dashed line on the ruler and cut on the right side of the ruler. Make a straight cut. Because you are cutting on a folded strip, each cut will make a set of mirror-image triangles. Square up left edge of the fabric and repeat Step 2.

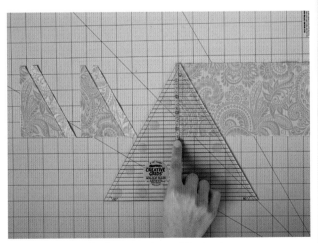

Cutting mirror-image 30° triangles

TRAPEZOIDS

1. Cut a strip of fabric the width specified in the pattern directions. The photo example shows a 1½" strip.

2. Lay the Creative Grids 60° Triangle ruler on top of the strip, with the top of the triangle extending above the strip as shown. Place the 3¼" measurement for the piece on the *bottom* edge of the fabric strip. Cut along both the left and right sides of the triangle ruler.

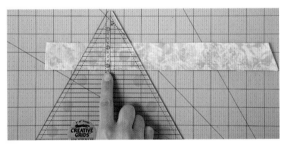

Cut first trapezoid.

3. Rotate the triangle ruler and place the 3¼" measurement on the *top* edge of the fabric strip. Cut along the right side of the triangle ruler. Continue to rotate the triangle ruler and cut more trapezoids.

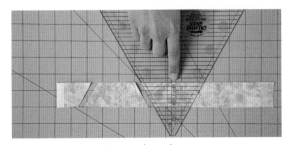

Rotate ruler and cut.

CUTTING FROM LAYERS

This technique is used in the first pattern in this book, *Stacking Birds* (page 17). It is a quick and easy way to create a design within triangles by taking advantage of the design on the fabric. Unlike fussy cutting—in which you place a template on one design motif, cut, then move to the next identical motif, and so on—this technique allows you to cut multiple identical pieces at once by aligning the printed motif on several layers of fabric and cutting strips through all the layers. You can then cut identical pieces from the strips. This stacking method saves both fabric and time.

Following are steps for creating five identical shapes from layers of fabric. This method is based on finding the *design repeats*; the size of the repeat is the distance along the selvage from the start of a design motif to the point where that motif appears again.

1. Cut 1 strip of fabric that is the width of the repeat by half the width of the fabric. This piece will be your guide for cutting the next pieces. Cut the number of strips needed for the project.

2. Stack and align the layers. Choose a motif you want to feature in the triangle. Carefully place a pin vertically through all the layers at the same spot, so the same motif is lined up in each layer. Repeat across the strip length.

Place pin through same spot on each layer.

3. Insert another pin through all the layers as shown. Then remove the first pin; the second pin will keep the layers from shifting.

Second pin keeps fabrics from shifting.

4. Use a ruler and rotary cutter to cut a strip the width given in the pattern directions, through all the layers. Now you're ready to subcut the strip into specific shapes, such as the triangle shown here. As you cut each triangle stack, keep those triangles together so you can use the triangles from the same stack all in the same star when you are ready to lay out the quilt.

Stack of shapes for desired pattern

CUTTING FROM STRIP SETS

Cutting from strip sets greatly speeds up the cutting process. From these sets you will cut diamonds, triangles, or templates. Note that the order and direction in which you arrange and sew the strips will determine the pattern of the units/shapes when you sew them together.

Making a strip set

When a strip set is needed in a project, specific instructions will be given for the strip widths and arrangement of the strips for the particular project. Here's how a strip set can be constructed:

Place the first strip on your cutting mat, right side up. Then place the second strip beneath the first strip; offset the left end by the width of the strip as shown in the photo. Repeat for strips 3 and 4. Pin the long edges of the strips right sides together, stitch with a scant ¼" seam, and press the seams toward the darker fabric.

Pin and sew strips together in their proper order.

Cutting diamonds

To cut diamonds, you will need a regular rotary ruler.

1. The first cut will be a 60°-angle cut. To achieve this, place the strip set edge parallel to the bottom edge of a horizontal gridline on your cutting mat. Place the ruler on top of the fabric, aligning the ruler's 60° line with the horizontal line on the mat. Cut along the left edge of the ruler. This initial cut will create the first edge of the diamond unit.

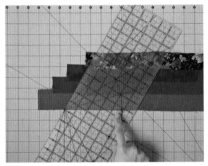

60°-angle cut on strip set

2. For the desired strip set width, refer to the project instructions. This example shows a 5¼" diamond. Use a ruler to measure the width from the first cut edge, keeping the ruler at the same 60° angle. Make the next cut along the right side of the ruler. You can see the diamond shape through the acrylic ruler. Repeat along the length of the strip set to make the number of cuts required for the project.

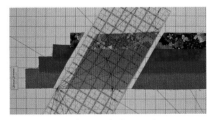

Cutting diamonds from strip set

Cutting triangles

You may use the pattern template provided or you may use the Creative Grids 60° Triangle ruler to cut triangles from strip sets.

1. For the desired triangle size, use the Creative Grids 60° Triangle ruler. Place the triangle on top of the fabric, lining up the size indicated on the pattern with the number on the ruler to match the bottom edge of the fabric. This example shows a 5¼" triangle. Cut along the left and right edges of the triangle.

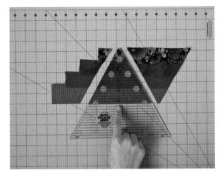

Cutting triangle from strip set

2. Rotate the triangle and use the top edge of the fabric for the measurement indicated on the pattern. Continue to cut triangles across the fabric.

Cutting templates

Place the project template on the strip set, matching up the lines on the template with the seamlines and matching the dark and light fabrics according to the template. Cut around the template.

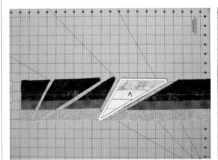 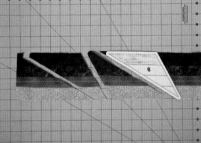

Unique A and B templates cut from strip set

Essential Techniques

The quilt projects in this book are made using several techniques, including appliqué, Y-seams for piecing triangles, and overlays to create value changes. These techniques are presented in this section, along with techniques for mitering quilt borders and for creating special borders for the hexagon-shaped quilts in this book.

Y-SEAMS

Star Shuffle (page 48) is a good example of a quilt with lots of Y-seams.

The Y-seam, also called a set-in seam, is required for sewing three pieces of fabric that come together at the same point. This point must be marked exactly with a dot ¼" from the cut edges of each fabric section. In the example shown, pieces A and B are sewn together first; then C is added. Some Y-seams have unequal angles, but in this book we will be working with the 120° Y-seam, so all three angles are the same. Therefore, it doesn't actually matter in what order you sew the seams. The following steps will make the process of creating a triangle with Y-seams easy.

1. Lay out the A, B, and C pieces needed for sewing the Y-seam and, with a fabric marker, mark dots ¼" in where the center of the Y-seam will meet on each piece. To position and mark the dots, I use the Perfect Piecer and a Chaco Liner pen (see Supplies, page 6). These markers come in different colors. Marking the dots accurately is crucial for the piecing to be successful.

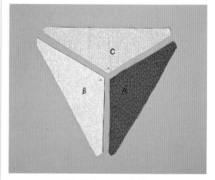

Mark dots precisely.

2. Flip triangle A onto triangle B with right sides together. Place a pin through the matching dots on pieces A and B. Start sewing at the pin at the dot. Tack with 3 small stitches. Then continue sewing to the end of the fabric.

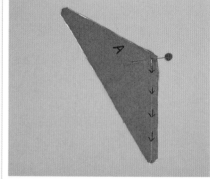

Start sewing right at dot.

3. Open the pieces and press the seam toward A.

4. Flip triangle C onto triangle A. Pin through the matching dots. Make sure all the seams are out of the way, so you will be sewing through only 2 layers of fabric. Start sewing at the dot. Tack with 3 small stitches, and then continue to the end of the fabric.

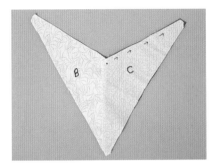

Sew C to A.

5. Open the pieces and press the seam toward C. Now you are ready to sew the last leg of the Y-seam. Fold the unit in half, with the right sides of B and C together. Make sure all the seams are out of the way to sew on only 2 layers of fabric. Tack with 3 small stitches. Then continue sewing to the end of the fabric.

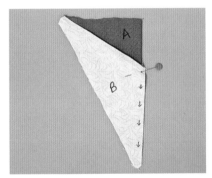

Secure stitches at dot.

6. Open the piece and press the seam toward B. From the back of the piece, all the seams should be pressed clockwise.

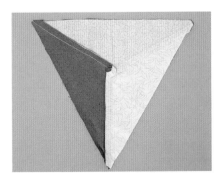

Seams pressed clockwise

APPLIQUÉ

This fusible appliqué technique is used in *My Flower Garden* (page 59). You will appliqué the quilt pieces before you sew them into the quilt blocks.

Trace the appliqué pattern provided for the project on one side of double-sided fusible web. Roughly cut out the shape ¼" larger than the pattern. Peel the unmarked paper off the back and follow the manufacturer's instructions to fuse the web onto the wrong side of the desired fabric. Cut out the fabric on the pattern line. Peel off the remaining paper. Place the fabric shape on the chosen background and fuse it in position. Stitch it on using your favorite machine appliqué stitch, tacking at the beginning and end with a small straight stitch.

OVERLAYS

This technique is used in *Dazzling Daisies* (page 54). You will apply the overlay to the pieces before they are sewn into quilt blocks.

An overlay is a shape cut from a dark shade of nylon netting, organdy, or any sheer fabric, which you place over another fabric to create a deeper shade of color. It is an easy way to achieve another value of a fabric you already have. Place the desired overlay over the piece of fabric. Stitch a scant ¼″ around the edge of fabric. This will hold the overlay in place and keep it from slipping around. In some cases where appliqué is used on top of the overlay, it will not be necessary to stitch around the outer edge of the piece.

MITERED BORDERS

A quilt can have one mitered border or several mitered borders. If you are making a quilt that has three borders, for example, sew the three border strips together along their lengths to make one wide border. This wider border section is treated as a single border piece when you add it as a mitered border.

Here is the mitered border length formula for the projects in this book:

Length of quilt side + 2 complete unfinished border widths + 2″ = Border length

1. To determine the average length of the top and bottom border piece, take 3 measurements—across the quilt top, across the middle, and across the bottom. Follow the border length formula to determine the border length. Prepare 2 strips to this measurement, sewing strips end to end as needed. Place pins at the center of each border length, and mark the width of the quilt with pins, measuring from the center pin on each border strip.

2. To determine the side border piece lengths, repeat Step 1, measuring through the vertical center and sides and adding the additional measurements. Follow the border length formula to determine the side border length. Prepare 2 strips to this measurement, sewing strips end to end as needed. Place pins at the center of each border length, and mark the width of the quilt with pins, measuring from the center pin on each border strip.

3. Pin mark the center of each side of the quilt. Pin the border strips to the quilt, matching the centers and quilt corners to the pins. Pin as often as needed to work in any fullness. Sew each border strip to the quilt, beginning and ending the seam ¼″ from the quilt top corners. Tack with 3 small stitches at the start and end of each sewing line.

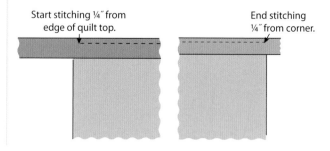

4. Fold the quilt corner with right sides together. Press the seams toward the quilt. (They can be pressed toward the border later.) Place a ruler on top of the folded corner. Mark a 45° sewing line, starting where the stitching stopped when the borders were sewn on. If the border is pieced, pin at each border intersection. Sew along this line.

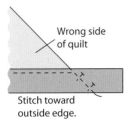

5. Look at the quilt corner from the right side to make sure it has a 90° angle. Trim the seams to ¼″ and press the seams open.

Mitered borders for hexagonal quilts

Bursting Forth (page 36)

Some of the quilts in this book finish to hexagonal shapes. To add mitered borders to these quilts, follow the same basic steps as for regular mitered borders, but with the variations that follow.

Again, here is the mitered border length formula for the projects in this book:

Length of quilt side + 2 complete unfinished border widths + 2″ = Border length

1. Mark the center of each quilt side with a pin. Measure the sides of the quilt top, starting and stopping ¼″ in from the corners. Take the average of all 6 sides. Follow the border length formula to determine the border length. Prepare 6 border strips to this measurement. Pin mark this length on each border section, measuring from the border center. Align the border edge with the quilt edge, right sides together, matching the centers of the border and the side. Pin the border in place, starting in the center and pinning to ¼″ from the corner of the quilt. Sew it in place, stopping and starting ¼″ from the quilt corners.

2. To miter the corner, follow Step 4 under Mitered Borders (at left), except the fold of the fabric creates a 60° line. Fold the quilt corner with right sides together. Press the seams toward the quilt. (They can be pressed toward the border later.) Place a ruler on top of the folded corner. Mark a 60° sewing line, starting where the stitching stopped when the borders were sewn on. If the border is pieced, pin at each border intersection. Sew along this line. Trim the seam to ¼″ and press the seam open.

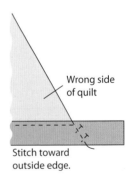

TRIANGLES TO STARS

Under the Stars, 38″ × 41″,
made and machine quilted by Barbara Cline

This section features quilts in which triangles are used to create star designs, from very simple to more complex. In the first project, **Stacking Birds** *(page 17), you will use a template to cut out simple triangles that form the star. Stacking the fabrics and fussy cutting them gives a new dimension to the design. Starting with* **Fall Stars** *(page 21), the pattern from which* **Under the Stars** *was made, you will piece triangles before sewing the triangles into rows. Look closely at how a star is created with the different components of a triangle.*

Strip piecing is another technique that is used in this chapter. In **Bursting Forth** *(page 36) you will be using Y-seam construction as well as learning to apply overlays to create a three-dimensional effect. This quilt is also made in a hexagon shape.* **Twinkle, Twinkle Little Star** *(page 43) is more involved because the piecing is smaller. And last but not least,* **Star Shuffle** *(page 48) combines strip piecing, Y-seams, and many points coming together.*

Made and machine quilted by Barbara Cline

Finished size: *42″ × 47″*

Of all the quilts in this book, this one is the easiest to make. It is composed of simple triangles that are fussy cut in strips to make use of the fabric design. You subcut strips into triangles, sew the triangles into rows, and then sew together the rows to construct the quilt. What creates the sense of movement in the quilt is the placement of the colors to form stars as well as the design created within the star.

Pick two fabrics that have a design repeat of 7″ or more. Refer to Cutting from Layers (page 10). Be aware that these two fabrics need to be completely different in pattern, color, and value. It is good if one of them is bold, bright, and lively and the other is less bold, with less motion in the print.

Materials

Yardage is based on 42″-wide fabric with a repeat of 7″ or more.

- **Black print:** ⅝ yard, plus 5 pattern repeats for stars and border
- **Yellow print:** ⅝ yard, plus 5 pattern repeats for stars, borders, and binding
- **Light gray fabric:** ⅞ yard for background
- **Backing fabric:** 2¾ yards
- **Batting:** 48″ × 53″
- **Template plastic**
- **Creative Grids 60° Triangle ruler** (optional)

Cutting

Copy Stacking Birds templates A and B (page 84) at 100%. Refer to Using Templates (page 7) to cut the indicated triangles. [Optional: Refer to Using the Creative Grids 60° Triangle ruler (page 8) to cut the pieces with the ruler; use the measurements given in the brackets.]

First cut:

From the black and yellow fabrics, first cut each lengthwise on the center fold. Save one side for cutting borders; from the other side cut 5 strips the width of the design repeat. Stack the 5 strips as described in Cutting from Layers (page 10). Then proceed with the rest of the cuts.

Black:

- Cut the stack of strips to 5½″-wide strips; subcut into 30 triangles [5½″] using template A. Make 6 stacks of 5 triangles.

- Cut 4 strips 2½″ × 52″.

Yellow:

- Cut the stack of strips to 5½″-wide strips; subcut into 30 triangles [5½″] using template A. Make 6 stacks of 5 triangles.

- Cut 4 strips 2¼″ × LOF.*

- Cut 8 strips 1¼″ × 52″.

Light gray:

- Cut 3 strips 5½″ × WOF*; subcut into 28 triangles [5½″] using template A.

- Cut 2 strips 5½″ × WOF*; subcut into 8 triangles using template B and 8 triangles using template Br [8 sets of mirror-image 30° triangles 5½″].

LOF = length of fabric; WOF = width of fabric

Assembling the Quilt Top

1. Refer to the quilt layout diagram to lay out the complete quilt top before sewing anything. Using one stack of triangles, position the fussy-cut triangles so that the fabric motif creates a design in the center of each star. Use another stack of triangles for the outside of each star.

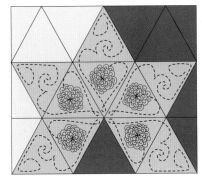

Star layout

2. Sew together each row and press; then sew the rows together and press. Alternate the pressing direction from row to row. Stitch a scant ¼″ around the edge of the quilt top. This will keep the edges of the quilt from stretching.

tip

When sewing rows together, sew 2 rows at a time. Pin a complete row together and then pin the next row together. Place a pin at the end of the row, pointing in the direction the seam is to be pressed. Place 2 pins in next (indicating row 2), pointing in the opposite direction, showing which way to press the seams. When sewing the rows together, you will know to press the seam in the direction the pins are pointed.

3. Sew a black 2½″ strip between 2 yellow 1¼″ strips for each side of the quilt. Refer to Mitered Borders (page 14) to sew these border units to the quilt.

Quilt layout

4. Use your favorite methods to layer, quilt, and bind the quilt with the 2¼″ strips. I quilted the background with a simple diagonal grid, and the stars are echo quilted with star designs.

Quilting detail

My Man's Tricks, 41″ × 46″, made and machine quilted by Barbara Cline

This quilt is a variation of the *Stacking Birds* pattern. Notice that three different fabrics are used for the stars instead of two. In addition, cording is zigzagged on top of the quilt with a transparent thread around the stars.

Quilting detail

LIFE LESSONS

by Parla Sonifrank
(the author's daughter)

Over the years, I have come to love the art of sewing because of the way in which I have seen it pull my family together. I actually do not enjoy sewing that much, but the one time during the year that I love to sew is during my family's annual sewing retreat. Every year, my grandmother, mom, aunts, and cousins get together for ten days, just to spend time with each other and to sew.

Some of them absolutely love to sew, some enjoy it a bit, and some bring other kinds of projects to work on—but it is the art of sewing that brings us together, and that is what I love the most about it!

Through sewing, I have come to see the way in which my family members value each other and me. I love how my aunts interact with each other and with the younger generations, and I am always excited about an opportunity to spend time with my cousins. It could have been scrapbooking; it could have been basket-weaving or painting—but it is sewing that brings us together every year, and I love it for that!

Made and machine quilted by Barbara Cline

Finished size: 41″ × 45″

The stars in this quilt are made with two different triangle designs. Each star has two values (dark and medium) of the same color to create a strong contrasting "border" around the star. The quilt has three borders; triangles using all the star fabrics add interest to the middle border, which is placed between two cream borders. The binding is made up of strips cut from all the star fabrics.

Materials

Yardage is based on 42"-wide fabric.

FOR STARS, PIECED BORDER, AND BINDING:

- **Dark brown:** ½ yard
- **Medium brown:** ½ yard
- **Dark orange:** ½ yard
- **Medium orange:** ½ yard
- **Dark green:** ½ yard
- **Medium green:** ½ yard

FOR BACKGROUND AND BORDERS:

- **Cream:** 1½ yards

OTHER:

- **Backing fabric:** 2⅝ yards
- **Batting:** 47" × 51"
- **Template plastic**
- **Creative Grids 60° Triangle ruler** (optional)

Cutting

Copy Fall Stars templates A–G (pages 74 and 75) at 100%. Refer to Using Templates (page 7) to cut the indicated pieces. Label all the pieces with the given letters. [Optional: Refer to Using the Creative Grids 60° Triangle ruler (page 8) to cut the triangles and trapezoids with the ruler; use the measurements given in brackets.]

Dark brown:

- Cut 2 strips 2" × WOF;* subcut into 34 triangles [2"] using template A. These are A pieces.
- Cut 1 strip 2" × WOF; subcut into 10 trapezoids [3½"] using template C. These are C pieces.
- Cut 2 strips 2" × WOF; subcut into 10 trapezoids [5"] using template D. These are D pieces.
- Cut 1 strip 2¼" × WOF.

Medium brown:

- Cut 1 strip 2" × WOF; subcut into 24 triangles [2"] using template A. These are A pieces.
- Cut 2 strips 3½" × WOF; subcut into 10 pieces using template B. These are B pieces.
- Cut 1 strip 2¼" × WOF.

Dark orange:

- Cut 2 strips 2" × WOF; subcut into 34 triangles [2"] using template A. These are A pieces.
- Cut 1 strip 2" × WOF; subcut into 10 trapezoids [3½"] using template C. These are C pieces.
- Cut 2 strips 2" × WOF; subcut into 10 trapezoids [5"] using template D. These are D pieces.
- Cut 1 strip 2¼" × WOF.

Medium orange:

- Cut 1 strip 2" × WOF; subcut into 24 triangles [2"] using template A. These are A pieces.
- Cut 2 strips 3½" × WOF; subcut into 10 pieces using template B. These are B pieces.
- Cut 1 strip 2¼" × WOF.

Dark green:

▦ Cut 2 strips 2″ × WOF; subcut into 34 triangles [2″] using template A. These are A pieces.

▦ Cut 1 strip 2″ × WOF; subcut into 10 trapezoids [3½″] using template C. These are C pieces.

▦ Cut 2 strips 2″ × WOF; subcut into 10 trapezoids [5″] using template D. These are D pieces.

▦ Cut 1 strip 2¼″ × WOF.

Medium green:

▦ Cut 1 strip 2″ × WOF; subcut into 24 triangles [2″] using template A. These are A pieces.

▦ Cut 2 strips 3½″ × WOF; subcut into 10 pieces using template B. These are B pieces.

▦ Cut 1 strip 2¼″ × WOF.

Cream:

▦ Cut 4 strips 2″ × WOF; subcut into 80 triangles [2″] using template A and 4 triangles using template G and 4 triangles using template Gr [4 sets of mirror-image 30° triangles].

▦ Cut 3 strips 5″ × WOF; subcut into 28 triangles [5″] using template E. These are E pieces.

▦ Cut 2 strips 5″ × WOF; subcut into 8 triangles using template F and 8 triangles using template Fr [8 sets of mirror-image 30° triangles 5″]. These are F and Fr pieces.

▦ Cut 8 strips 2″ × WOF.

▦ Cut 4 squares 2″ × 2″.

WOF = width of fabric

Making the Triangles

The stars are made up of two simple pieced triangles.

1. To make a triangle 1 unit, sew 2 of dark piece A's to a medium piece B as shown. Press seams toward A. Make 10 brown, 10 orange, and 10 green triangle 1 units.

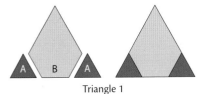

Triangle 1

2. To make a triangle 2 unit, sew 1 medium piece A to 1 dark piece C; add a dark piece D as shown. Press the seams toward A. Make 10 brown, 10 orange, and 10 green triangle 2 units.

Triangle 2

Assembling the Quilt Top

Arrange the triangle 1 and 2 units with the cream triangles E, F, and Fr to form 8 rows as shown in the quilt layout diagram. Sew each row together, pressing the seams in alternate directions from row to row. Then sew the rows together. Press. Stitch a scant ¼″ around the edge of the quilt top. This will keep the edges from stretching.

Quilt layout

Adding the Borders

1. Use 4 cream 2″ strips for the first border. Measure the quilt through the vertical center and cut 2 side border strips to this measurement. Sew these to the sides. Press the seams toward the border. Measure the quilt through the horizontal center and cut 2 border strips to this measurement. Sew these to the top and bottom of the quilt.

2. To make the triangle border, use the remaining A pieces. Use cream triangles between colored triangles. Always keep the colored triangle points facing the same direction. For the quilt sides, sew 21 cream triangles between 22 colored triangles. Add a cream triangle (G or Gr) from a mirror-image triangle set to each end. Press. Make 2 rows. Sew these to the quilt sides. Press the seams toward the first border.

3. Make 2 rows with 19 cream triangles between 20 colored triangles and add a cream triangle from a mirror-image triangle set to each end. Then add a 2″ cream square to the ends of each row. Press. Sew these to the top and bottom of the quilt. Press the seams toward the first border.

4. Repeat Step 1 to complete the final border, using the remaining cream 2″ strips.

5. Use your favorite methods to layer and quilt the quilt top. Using variegated thread, I quilted a simple diagonal grid creating triangles on the background fabric; on the center part of the stars I quilted feathers; and on the darker part of the stars I quilted a continuous loop pattern.

Quilting detail

6. To make the binding, sew together the 2¼″ strips end to end in a pleasing sequence of colors and bind the quilt using your favorite method. You may want to trim some of the binding strips to be shorter than the WOF so that you can use all the colors in the binding.

Scrappy Stars, 41" × 43", made and machine quilted by Barbara Cline

In this variation, I wanted to use all scraps. Notice that the background is made up of different light-value fabrics in all the colors represented in the stars. The yellow adds some sparkle and zip to the quilt. The arrangement of pieces creates a new star behind the smaller star. This one has plain borders.

Under the Stars, 38" × 41", made and machine quilted by Barbara Cline

This quilt is another color variation of *Fall Stars;* it features the triangle borders like those in the main project.

LIFE LESSONS

By Rebecca Cline
(the author's daughter)

I remember visiting my aunt and uncle's home one summer with my cousin Hannah. One of the things my aunt asked us to do was make a comforter. Hannah and I hated every second of it. We sewed as fast as we could so that we could be done with that awful comforter that encroached on our playtime. I just knew that I would always hate sewing because of that comforter. A few years later, Mom told my sisters and me that we were each allowed to take one sewing class at Patchwork Plus. I enrolled in a pillow-making class with Hannah. We both had so much fun making our pillows, and we both still have them. I know that Mom could have taught us what we learned in that class, but she let us take the classes because she thought that we would have more fun. She tried her hardest to make sewing fun for her daughters in hopes that one day we would pick it up for ourselves. And, contrary to my belief that I would always hate sewing, somewhere along the way I learned to love it.

TUMBLING STARS

Made and machine quilted by Barbara Cline

Finished size: 58″ × 60″

To create this sparkling quilt you will want to pick tone-on-tone prints that don't have a lot of pattern to them. You will need sixteen fabrics—two shades each (a dark and a light) of eight colors. Notice that in the border, all the fabrics are used; this gives the quilt a nice finished touch.

Materials

Yardage is based on 42"-wide fabric.

- **Fabrics:** 16 colors, ½ yard each, for stars and pieced border:
Light gray, dark gray; light purple, dark purple; light teal, dark teal; light green, dark green; light lavender, dark lavender; light lime, dark lime; light burgundy, dark burgundy; light plum, dark plum

- **Gray fabric:** 2¼ yards for background, outside border, and binding

- **Backing fabric:** 3⅝ yards

- **Batting:** 64" × 66"

- **Template plastic**

- **Creative Grids 60° Triangle ruler** (optional)

Cutting

Copy Tumbling Stars templates A–E (pages 76 and 77) at 100%. Refer to Using Templates (page 7) to cut the indicated pieces. Label all the pieces with the given letter. [Optional: Refer to Using the Creative Grids 60° Triangle ruler (page 8) to cut the pieces with the ruler; use the measurements given in brackets.]

Lights and darks of gray, purple, and teal:

- Cut 1 strip 3¾" × WOF;* subcut into 10 triangles [3¾"] using template A. These are A pieces.

- Cut 2 strips 1½" × WOF; subcut into 10 trapezoids [5¾"] using template C. These are C pieces.

- Cut 2 strips 1½" × WOF; subcut into 14 trapezoids [4¾"] using template B. These are B pieces.

Lights and darks of green, lavender, and burgundy:

- Cut 1 strip 3¾" × WOF; subcut into 8 triangles [3¾"] using template A. These are A pieces.

- Cut 2 strips 1½" × WOF; subcut into 8 trapezoids [5¾"] using template C. These are C pieces.

- Cut 2 strips 1½" × WOF; subcut into 12 trapezoids [4¾"] using template B. These are B pieces.

Lights and darks of lime green and plum:

- Cut 1 strip 3¾" × WOF; subcut into 6 triangles [3¾"] using template A. These are A pieces.

- Cut 1 strip 1½" × WOF; subcut into 6 trapezoids [5¾"] using template C. These are C pieces.

- Cut 2 strips 1½" × WOF; subcut into 10 trapezoids [4¾"] using template B. These are B pieces.

Gray:

- Cut 5 strips 5¾" × WOF; subcut into 38 triangles [5¾"] using template D. These are D pieces.

- Cut 2 strips 5¾" × WOF; subcut into 10 triangles using template E and 10 triangles using template Er [10 sets of mirror-image 30° triangles 5¾"]. These are pieces E and F.

- Cut 14 strips 2¼" × WOF.

*WOF = width of fabric

Making the Triangles

1. With an A triangle, a B trapezoid, and a C trapezoid, make the following triangle. Sew the B trapezoid to the right side of A, and then sew the C trapezoid to the left side of A as shown. Press seams toward A.

2. Repeat Step 1 to complete the following units:

- 10 with dark gray triangles and light gray trapezoids

- 10 with light gray triangles and dark gray trapezoids

- 10 with dark purple triangles and light purple trapezoids

- 10 with light purple triangles and dark purple trapezoids

- 10 with dark teal triangles and light teal trapezoids

- 10 with light teal triangles and dark teal trapezoids

- 8 with dark green triangles and light green trapezoids

- 8 with light green triangles and dark green trapezoids

- 8 with dark lavender triangles and light lavender trapezoids

- 8 with light lavender triangles and dark lavender trapezoids

- 8 with dark burgundy triangles and light burgundy trapezoids

- 8 with light burgundy triangles and dark burgundy trapezoids

- 6 with dark lime green triangles and light lime green trapezoids

- 6 with light lime green triangles and dark lime green trapezoids

- 6 with dark plum triangles and light plum trapezoids

- 6 with light plum triangles and dark plum trapezoids

Assembling the Quilt Top

Lay out the triangles according to the quilt layout diagram. Sew the triangles into vertical rows and then join the rows. Press the seams in alternate directions from row to row. Stitch a scant ¼″ around the edge of the quilt top. This will keep the edges of the quilt from stretching.

Quilt layout

Adding the Borders

1. Sew together the remaining B trapezoids to form the first border as shown in the quilt layout diagram. Press. Make 4 strips 63″ long. Trim the ends as needed.

2. Sew 2¼″ gray strips end to end to make a 63″ border strip. Repeat to make 4.

3. Sew the trapezoid border strips to the gray border strips and refer to Mitered Borders (page 14) to sew them to the quilt top.

4. Use your favorite methods to layer, quilt, and bind the quilt. I quilted a diagonal grid in the background and individual leaf motifs surrounded with stippling in each diamond shape.

Quilting detail

LIFE LESSONS

by Autumn Cline
(the author's daughter)

When I was eleven or twelve, I decided that I wanted to make a blanket. I started out full-force, ready to do anything and everything. I soon found out that speed was definitely not everything. My mom told me to slow down and make sure that I had my edges lined up and that my thread was okay. I ignored her advice and ended up picking out a lot of my work. This was super frustrating, but even after that, I still had not learned my lesson. I went right back at it, full speed ahead! I wanted the finished product but did not want to put in the effort that was needed to complete it well. Thanks to my impatience and carelessness, I ended up sewing for a really long time without realizing that my thread had run out! What a bummer! This time I learned my lesson and worked harder to make sure I did it right the first time. My mom helped me out like a good mother would, and I did the rest with care. I guess the old adage is true—haste makes waste!

SHENANDOAH STARS

Pieced by Polly Yoder and quilted by Margaret Wade

Finished size: 99″ × 112″

This is a large quilt, but it goes together rather quickly because the units—diamonds and triangles—are cut from strip sets. This quilt looks like it would be complicated to piece because of the octagon shapes surrounding the stars. But look beyond the octagons and you see that they are made up of large triangles, which are themselves pieced from a diamond and two smaller triangles; there are no Y-seams. To piece the quilt, these triangles are simply sewn into rows.

The quilt's sparkle is achieved with the placement of the complementary colors—the bright yellow triangles on either side of the darker blue diamonds, and the little yellow pinwheels in the star centers.

When you make the strip-pieced triangles for this quilt, you will have some left over. If you wish, you can make a pillowcase to match the quilt, using the pillowcase instructions (page 34).

Materials

Yardage is based on 42"-wide fabric.

- **Light blue:** 1⅛ yards for diamonds

- **Medium-light blue:** 2⅜ yards total (1⅛ yards for diamonds and 1¼ yards for first and third borders)

- **Medium blue:** 4⅜ yards total (1⅛ yards for diamonds and 3¼ yards for second and fourth borders)

- **Dark blue:** 1¼ yards for diamonds

- **Dark green:** ⅞ yard for triangles

- **Green print:** ⅞ yard for triangles

- **Medium green:** 1¾ yards for triangles

- **Yellow-green:** 2¼ yards for triangles and pinwheels

- **Bright yellow:** 1½ yards for triangles

- **Binding:** 1 yard

- **Backing fabric:** 9 yards

- **Batting:** 107" × 120"

- **Template plastic**

- **Creative Grids 60° Triangle ruler** (optional)

Cutting

Copy Shenandoah templates A and C (page 78) at 200%. Copy template B (page 78) at 100%. Refer to Using Templates (page 7). These templates will be used in the construction steps. [Optional: Refer to Using the Creative Grids 60° Triangle ruler (page 8) to cut the pieces with the ruler; use the measurements given in brackets.]

Light blue:
- Cut 14 strips 2½" × WOF.*

Medium-light blue:
- Cut 14 strips 2½" × WOF.
- Cut 24 strips 1½" × WOF.

Medium blue:
- Cut 14 strips 2½" × WOF.
- Cut 4 strips 2½" × LOF.*
- Cut 4 strips 4½" × LOF.

Dark blue:
- Cut 14 strips 2½" × WOF.

Dark green:
- Cut 9 strips 2½" × WOF.

Green print:
- Cut 9 strips 2½" × WOF.

Medium green:
- Cut 21 strips 2½" × WOF.

Yellow-green:

▦ Cut 21 strips 2½″ × WOF.

▦ Cut 7 strips 3″ × WOF; subcut into a total of 27 rectangles 3″ × 8¼″; subcut each on the diagonal for a total of 54 triangles for the pinwheels. (When you cut the triangles, have the fabric right side up and always cut from the top left to the bottom right.)

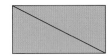

Bright yellow:

▦ Cut 18 strips 2½″ × WOF.

Binding:

▦ Cut 11 strips 2¼″ × WOF.

WOF = width of fabric; LOF = length of fabric

Making the Diamonds

1. Using 2½″-wide strips to make the diamonds, refer to Cutting from Strip Sets (page 10) to assemble a strip set in the color order shown, but offset each new strip 1½″ from the end of the previous strip. Stitch scant ¼″ seams and press the seams toward the dark fabrics. Repeat to make 14 strip sets.

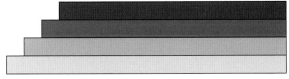

Lay out strip set.

2. Use a ruler to cut the strip sets into 60° diamonds that are 8½″ wide, referring to Cutting Diamonds (page 11). You will be able to cut 4 diamonds out of each strip set, for a total of 54 diamonds.

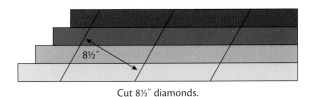

Cut 8½″ diamonds.

Making the Small Triangles

1. From the green and yellow fabrics, assemble strip sets in 2 different color orders as shown, offsetting each new strip 1½″ from the end of the previous strip. Stitch scant ¼″ seams and press toward the dark fabrics. Make 9 sets of each color arrangement.

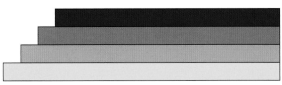

Set 1 fabric order: dark green, medium green, yellow-green, bright yellow. Make 9.

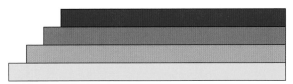

Set 2 fabric order: green print, medium green, yellow-green, bright yellow. Make 9.

2. Use template A to cut 8 triangles from each strip set. Rotate the template along the strip set. [Refer to Using the Creative Grids ruler (page 8) to cut 8 triangles 8½″ from each strip set.]

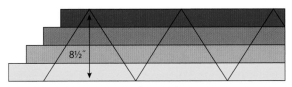

Cut 8 triangles from each strip set.

3. From the set 1 strips, you need a total of 12 unit A and 36 unit B triangles. You will have extra of unit A for the pillowcase project.

Unit A—Use 12.

Unit B—Use 36.

4. From the set 2 strips, you need a total of 24 unit C and 36 unit D triangles. You will have extra of unit C.

Unit C—Use 24.   Unit D—Use 36.

Making the Large Triangles

The octagon shape in this quilt is created with 6 large triangles. Each large triangle is made with 1 strip-pieced diamond, 2 strip-pieced triangles, and 1 small yellow triangle. They are made in 4 different combinations as shown.

1. Refer to the diagrams to make the indicated number of large triangles using the diamonds and the appropriate triangle units. Press the seams toward the diamond.

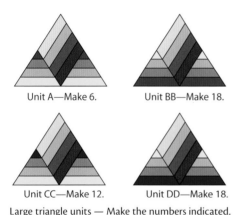

Unit A—Make 6.   Unit BB—Make 18.

Unit CC—Make 12.   Unit DD—Make 18.

Large triangle units — Make the numbers indicated.

2. Position template B on the front of a triangle as shown and trim off the top tip of each large triangle unit.

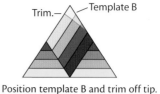

Trim.—   Template B

Position template B and trim off tip.

3. Position a yellow-green pinwheel piece on a large triangle as shown and sew in place. Press toward yellow-green.

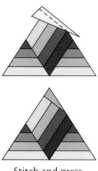

Stitch and press.

4. Using a rotary cutting ruler and a rotary cutter, trim off extra pinwheel fabric at the point of the triangle.

Making the Side Edge Units

1. Sew a yellow-green 2½″ strip to a medium green 2½″ strip. Make 3 strip sets.

2. Use template C to cut trapezoids [8½″] from the strip sets. As you move along the strips, rotate the template [ruler] to cut 5 trapezoids from each strip set for the side edge units. [Refer to Trapezoids (page 9) to cut 8½″ trapezoids.] You will have 3 extra edge units remaining after you lay out the quilt.

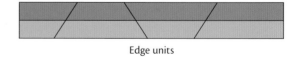

Edge units

Assembling the Quilt Top

1. Refer to the quilt center diagram to lay out the quilt top, noting the placement of the lettered large triangle units in the rows with the side edge pieces as shown. The hexagon shapes at the edges will be trimmed off after the rows are sewn together.

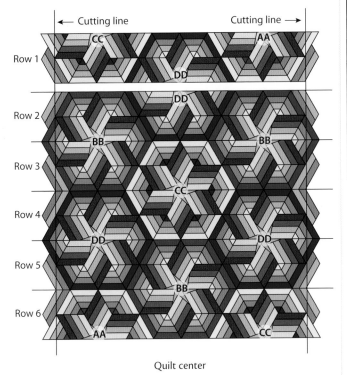

Quilt center

2. Sew the triangles and edge pieces into rows and press seams in alternate directions from row to row. Then sew the rows together as shown. Press. Trim off the edges to make a rectangle. Stitch a scant ¼" around the edge of the quilt top. This will keep the edges of the quilt from stretching.

3. Refer to Mitered Borders (page 14) to sew on the first (medium-light blue 1½" strips), second (medium blue 2½" strips), third (medium-light blue 1½" strips), and fourth (medium blue 4½" strips) borders as shown in the quilt layout diagram.

Quilt layout

4. Use your favorite methods to layer, quilt, and bind the quilt with the 2¼" strips. Margaret Wade, the quilter for this project, chose a meandering quilt design for the green and yellow hexagons and then stitched in-the-ditch for the stars.

Quilting detail

PILLOWCASE SET

Here's a simple pillowcase project you can make using the leftover triangles from the quilt project. This will make 2 pillowcases. Each pillowcase will finish 21″ × 32″.

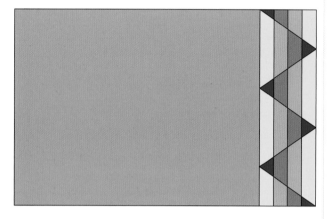

Materials

Yardage is based on 42″-wide fabric.

FOR A SET OF PILLOWCASES:

- **Light green:** 2 yards
- **Leftover unit A triangles:** 24

Cutting

Light green:

- Cut 2 strips 9″ × WOF.*
- Cut 2 strips 24½″ × WOF.

WOF = width of fabric

Making Each Pillowcase

1. Sew the 24 leftover unit A triangles into a long row. Then cut 2 sections, each 42″ long—1 strip for each pillowcase.

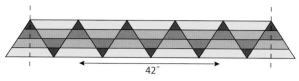

Cut sections 42″ long.

2. Sew a 9″ × WOF strip on one side of a triangle strip and a 24½″ strip on the other side of the strip. Press the seams toward the triangle strip.

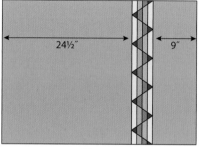

Assemble pillowcase.

3. Fold the pillowcase in half, right sides together, and sew the side and bottom seams. Serge or zigzag the raw edges of the seams and turn the pillowcase right side out.

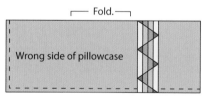

Sew side and bottom seams.

4. Press the raw edge of the top green section under ¼″. Then fold the top green section to the inside. Press the folded edge. Pin it in place and stitch in-the-ditch on the top of the pillowcase beside the bottom triangle strip, catching the turned-under fabric.

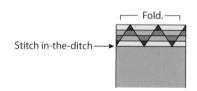

LIFE LESSONS

by Margaret Heatwole
(the author's mother)

I grew up in a home where my mother thought it was a waste of time and money to make quilts. She sewed to make and patch our clothes but did little else in the line of sewing. Because of this, I had no experience with quilting before I was married. But thankfully, I married into a quilting family! My mother-in-law invited me to her quilting bees where I was surrounded by very talented and experienced ladies. I would do anything to get out of quilting; I'd ask to help in the kitchen, wash dishes, or anything! But my mother-in-law was patient and just kept inviting me and showing me how to do those tiny stitches. One day I saw her inspecting my work. Her comment? "You've come a long way, baby!" That made my day, and I have now developed a true love for quilting.

BURSTING FORTH

Made and machine quilted by Barbara Cline

Finished size: 58″ × 50″

This project features overlays. Placing an overlay of organdy or netting over a fabric produces another value of that fabric's color. Here, overlays create depth in the stars and make them seem to jump out of the quilt. *Bursting Forth* is one of three hexagonal quilt projects in this book. The design, with its central star and the interesting shape, would make a dramatic wallhanging. You will have leftover triangles from this quilt; I've provided a bonus project, the *Simple Christmas Star (page 41)*, for you to make with them.

Materials

Yardage is based on 42"-wide fabric.

FOR STARS:

- **Light green:** ⅛ yard
- **Medium-light green:** ¼ yard
- **Medium green:** ½ yard
- **Dark green:** ⅜ yard
- **Light blue:** ⅛ yard
- **Medium-light blue:** ⅜ yard
- **Medium blue:** ½ yard
- **Dark blue:** ⅝ yard
- **Light red:** ¾ yard
- **Medium-light red:** ⅝ yard
- **Medium red:** ¾ yard

FOR OTHER:

- **Print fabric:** 1⅝ yards for border and binding
- **Backing fabric:** 3⅛ yards
- **Batting:** 64" × 56"
- **Black nylon netting:** 108" wide, ¾ yard for overlays
- **Template plastic**
- **Creative Grids 60° Triangle ruler** (optional)

Cutting

Copy the Bursting Forth templates A–G (pages 78 and 79) at 100%. Refer to Using Templates (page 7). Cut all template shapes with the fabric right side up. Refer to Cutting Diamonds (page 11). [Optional: Refer to Using the Creative Grids 60° Triangle ruler (page 8) to cut the pieces with the ruler; use the measurements given in the brackets.]

Print fabric:

- Cut 5 strips 1⅞" × WOF.*
- Cut 6 strips 3½" × WOF.
- Cut 6 strips 2¼" × WOF.

Light green:

- Cut 1 strip 2" × WOF; subcut into 9 diamonds using template A.

Medium-light green:

- Cut 1 strip 1¾" × WOF; subcut into 9 pieces using template B.
- Cut 1 strip 1¾" × WOF; subcut into 9 pieces using template Br.

Medium green:

- Cut 2 strips 1⅞" × WOF; subcut into 18 pieces using template C.
- Cut 1 strip 2⅛" × WOF; subcut into 9 pieces using template D.
- Cut 1 strip 2⅛" × WOF; subcut into 9 pieces using template Dr.

Dark green:

- Cut 1 strip 1⅞" × WOF; subcut into 18 triangles using template E.
- Cut 2 strips 1⅞" × WOF; subcut into 9 pieces using template F.
- Cut 2 strips 1⅞" × WOF; subcut into 9 pieces using template Fr.

Light blue:

- Cut 1 strip 2" × WOF; subcut into 15 diamonds using template A.

Medium-light blue:

- Cut 2 strips 1¾" × WOF; subcut into 15 pieces using template B.
- Cut 2 strips 1¾" × WOF; subcut into 15 pieces using template Br.

Medium blue:

- Cut 3 strips 1⅞" × WOF; subcut into 30 pieces using template C.
- Cut 2 strips 2⅛" × WOF; subcut into 15 pieces using template D.
- Cut 2 strips 2⅛" × WOF; subcut into 15 pieces using template Dr.

Dark blue:

- Cut 1 strip 1⅞" × WOF; subcut into 30 pieces using template E.
- Cut 3 strips 1⅞" × WOF; subcut into 15 pieces using template F.
- Cut 3 strips 1⅞" × WOF; subcut into 15 pieces using template Fr.

Light red:

- Cut 1 strip 2″ × WOF; subcut into 6 diamonds using template A.

- Cut 1 strip 1⅞″ × WOF; subcut into 12 pieces using template E.

- Cut 1 strip 1⅞″ × WOF; subcut into 6 pieces using template F.

- Cut 1 strip 1⅞″ × WOF; subcut into 6 pieces using template Fr.

- Cut 5 strips 1⅞″ × WOF.

Medium-light red:

- Cut 1 strip 1¾″ × WOF; subcut into 6 pieces using template B.

- Cut 1 strip 1¾″ × WOF; subcut into 6 pieces using template Br.

- Cut 5 strips 1⅞″ × WOF.

Medium red:

- Cut 2 strips 1⅞″ × WOF; subcut into 12 pieces using template C.

- Cut 1 strip 2⅛″ × WOF; subcut into 6 pieces using template D.

- Cut 1 strip 2⅛″ × WOF; subcut into 6 pieces using template Dr.

- Cut 5 strips 1⅞″ × WOF.

Nylon netting:

- Cut 3 strips 6½″ × WOF; subcut into 60 rectangles 4″ × 6½″.

*WOF = width of fabric

Making the Pieced Triangles

The stars feature 2 different triangle designs—unit A triangles and unit B triangles. Half of each unit has a netting overlay, which gives this project its dimensional effect.

Overlay gives dimensional effect.

UNIT A TRIANGLES

Unit A green triangle—Make 9.

Unit A blue triangle—Make 15.

Unit A red triangle—Make 6.

1. Lay out the pieces for each triangle unit before you begin sewing.

2. Begin with the green fabrics and sew together pieces B, C, and E. Press the seam toward B.

3. Sew together pieces Br, C, and E. Press the seam toward E.

4. Lay nylon netting over the Br/C/E unit and staystitch around the outer edges. Trim the nylon netting even with outside edges of the pieced unit.

5. Refer to Y-seams (page 12) to sew diamond A to the left and right units.

6. Follow Steps 1–5 to complete 9 green units A.

7. Follow Steps 1–5 to complete 15 blue units A.

8. Follow Steps 1–5 to complete 6 red units A. Note that in these red units, the E triangles are light red fabric.

UNIT B TRIANGLES

Unit B green triangle—Make 9.

Unit B blue triangle—Make 15.

Unit B red triangle—Make 6.

1. Lay out the pieces for each triangle unit before you begin sewing.

2. Begin with the green fabrics and sew D to F and press the seam toward D. Then sew Dr to Fr. Press the seam toward Fr.

3. Lay nylon netting over the Dr/Fr unit and staystitch around the outer edges. Trim the nylon netting even with outside edges of the pieced unit.

4. Sew together the D/F and Dr/Fr units. Press.

5. Follow Steps 1–4 to complete 9 green units B.

6. Follow Steps 1–4 to complete 15 blue units B.

7. Follow Steps 1–4 to complete 6 red units B. Note that in these red units, the F and Fr pieces are light red fabric.

Making Triangles and Diamonds from Strip Sets

In addition to the pieced template triangles, the stars and hexagonal borders feature triangles and diamonds cut from strip sets. For general cutting instructions, see Cutting from Strip Sets (page 10).

MAKING THE STRIP SETS

1. On your cutting mat, arrange the 1⅞"-wide strips in this order from top to bottom: light red, medium-light red, medium red, and print. Do not offset these strips from row to row.

2. Use scant ¼" seams to sew the strips together and press the seams toward the darker fabric. Repeat to make a total of 5 strip sets.

CUTTING THE DIAMONDS

From 3 of the strip sets you will cut 6 right diamonds and 6 left diamonds.

1. To cut the right diamonds, use your ruler to cut a 60° angle off the left side of the strip set. Place the ruler parallel to the 60° angle and make another cut 6" from the previous cut. Cut a total of 6 right diamonds.

6" right diamonds

2. To cut the left diamonds, use your ruler to cut the strip set at a 60° angle in the opposite direction. Place the ruler parallel to the 60° angle and make another cut 6" from the previous cut. Cut a total of 6 left diamonds.

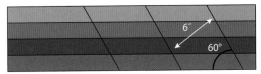

6" left diamonds

CUTTING THE TRIANGLES

From the remaining 2 strip sets, use template G to cut 10 triangles [6"], rotating the template [ruler] as you move along the strip. Cut 2 additional triangles [6"] from the remainder of the strip sets used to cut the diamonds.

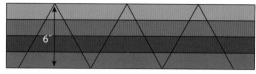

6" triangles

The triangles with the print fabric at the bottom are the ones you will use for this quilt. The other triangles can be used to make the *Simple Christmas Star* variation (page 41) or saved for another project.

Assembling the Quilt Top

Refer to the quilt layout diagram to position the units and rows before sewing.

Quilt layout

1. To create the center star, place 6 red unit A triangles in a circle with the diamonds in the center, and match 6 red unit B triangles to the red unit A triangles.

2. Add 5 blue unit A triangles around the top red unit B. Repeat on every other red star point. Match a blue unit B triangle to each blue unit A triangle.

3. At the remaining tips of the red star, add 3 green unit A triangles. Match a green unit B triangle to each of the green unit A triangles.

4. Add the left and right diamonds and the strip-pieced triangles as shown in the quilt layout diagram.

5. Sew the triangles and diamonds in diagonal rows as shown. Press the seams open.

6. Sew together the center rows and then add the 2 right rows and the 2 left rows. Press.

7. Refer to Mitered Borders for Hexagonal Quilts (page 15) to attach borders using the print 3½" strips.

8. Use your favorite methods to layer, quilt, and bind with the 2¼" strips. I decided to quilt a slight wave across the quilt. I echoed that line about 4 times; at the fifth line, halfway across the quilt, I created a new wave heading toward an edge and echoed that line 4 times. I kept repeating this idea over the whole quilt.

Quilting detail

SIMPLE CHRISTMAS STAR

This special bonus project was created to use up the scrap triangles from Bursting Forth. The finished size is 25″ × 22″.

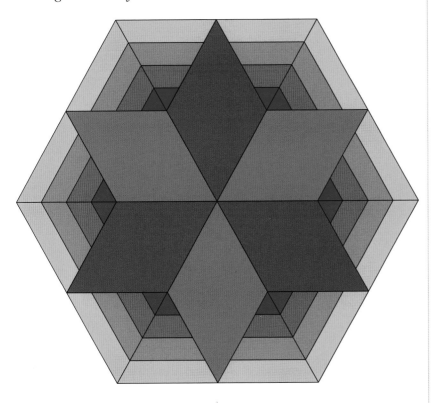

Materials

Yardage is based on 42″-wide fabric.

▥ **Green print:** ¾ yard for the star and binding

▥ **Nylon netting:** ¼ yard

▥ **Scrap triangles:** leftover from *Bursting Forth* (page 36)

▥ **Backing fabric:** 1 yard

▥ **Batting:** 31″ × 28″

Cutting

To cut the diamonds, refer to Cutting Diamonds (page 11).

Green print:
▥ Cut 2 strips 6″ × WOF;* subcut into 6 diamonds 6″.

▥ Cut 2 strips 2¼″ × WOF.

Nylon netting:
▥ Cut 1 strip 7″ × WOF; subcut into 3 diamonds 7″.

**WOF = width of fabric*

Assembling the Quilt Top

1. Refer to Overlays (page 14) to place and staystitch nylon netting over 3 of the green diamonds.

2. With the leftover triangles from *Bursting Forth* and the 6 green diamonds, create 6 large triangle units. Lay the netting overlays over 3 green diamonds. Sew each as shown. Press the seams toward the diamond.

Make 6.

3. Alternate the diamonds with the overlays to arrange the large triangle units in 2 rows. Sew each row together. Join the 2 rows. Press.

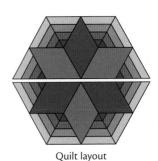

Quilt layout

4. Use your favorite methods to layer, quilt, and bind with the 2¼″ strips.

LIFE LESSONS

By June Flory
(the author's sister)

My sewing started at a very young age, with four scraps of feed-sack fabric that were marked with a cookie cutter. A bunny, a heart, a diamond, and a scalloped flower were marked with quarter-inch lines and spaces of equal length. My sewing consisted of running embroidery threads up at one end of the mark and down at the other end of the mark. This was the beginning of many successes because of the "I can't" lesson. I was never given a project about which I was allowed to say, "I can't." If those two words ever came out of my mouth, they were always countered with, "But of course you can!" from both my mother and my father. This lesson has carried on through every garment, quilt, interior decoration, art, remodeling, and craft project that I've worked on. Living with this lesson has opened the door to so many successes in life—from physical, hands-on projects to all matters of the heart, soul, and mind.

TWINKLE, TWINKLE
LITTLE STAR

Made and machine quilted by Barbara Cline

Finished size: 48″ × 42″

This quilt features smaller pieces, precision piecing, and a small star appliqué in the center. Notice how the border is placed behind the twinkling white stars to add an element of depth to the quilt. I used my stash for the cream background fabrics, but you could also use one cream fabric for the whole background. When you choose the three colors for each star, be sure to pick three different values. (There will be two slightly different values of the medium-value colors.) This will make the stars "twinkle"; otherwise, with the same values they will read as one colored spot.

Materials

Yardage is based on 42"-wide fabric.

Note that there are 4 values of each star color—1 dark, 2 slightly different mediums, and 1 light. This is because you will make some triangles using 1 medium value and some using the other.

- **Red print:** ⅝ yard for second border
- **Red I (medium value):** ¼ yard for stars
- **Red II (a little lighter than red I):** ⅛ yard for stars
- **Red III (dark value):** ⅛ yard for stars
- **Light red:** ⅜ yard for star background
- **Green I (medium value):** ⅛ yard for stars
- **Green II (a little lighter than green I):** ⅛ yard for stars
- **Green III (dark value):** ⅛ yard for stars
- **Light green:** ⅜ yard for star background
- **White I:** ⅝ yard for stars and binding
- **White II (a little darker than white I):** ⅜ yard for stars
- **White III (darker value):** ⅜ yard for stars (I used silver fabric.)
- **Cream fabric:*** 1⅛ yards total for background and border
- **Backing fabric:** 2¾ yards

- **Batting:** 54" × 48"
- **Double-sided fusible web:** 6" × 6" piece
- **Template plastic**
- **Creative Grids 60° Triangle ruler** (optional)

Use one cream fabric or several in assorted values.

Cutting

Copy Twinkle, Twinkle templates A–E and the Star (page 80) at 100%. Refer to Using Templates (page 7) to cut the indicated pieces. Label the pieces with the given letters. This will help you in assembling the quilt. [Optional: Refer to Using the Creative Grids 60° Triangle ruler (page 8) to cut the pieces with the ruler where the measurements are given in brackets.]

Red print:

- Cut 2 strips 4" × WOF;* subcut into 24 triangles [4"] using template E.
- Cut 1 strip 2¼" × WOF; subcut into 12 diamonds using template A. Label these A.
- Cut 1 strip 2¼" × WOF; subcut into 30 triangles using template B. Label these B.
- Cut 1 strip 2¼" × WOF; subcut into 30 triangles using template C. Label these C.

Red I:

- Cut 2 strips 2¼" × WOF; subcut into 9 pieces using template D (label these D), and 9 triangles using template C (label these E).

Red II:

- Cut 1 strip 2¼" × WOF; subcut into 6 pieces using template D (label these F), and 6 triangles using template C (label these G).

Red III:

- Cut 1 strip 2¼" × WOF; subcut into 15 triangles using template B (label these H), and 15 triangles using template C (label these I).

Light red:

- Cut 1 strip 2¼" × WOF; subcut into 15 diamonds using template A. Label these J.

Cut 1 strip 2¼″ × WOF; subcut into 30 triangles using template B. Label these K.

Cut 1 strip 2¼″ × WOF; subcut into 30 triangles using template C. Label these L.

Green I:

Cut 2 strips 2¼″ × WOF; subcut into 9 pieces using template D (label these M), and 9 triangles using template C (label these N).

Green II:

Cut 1 strip 2¼″ × WOF; subcut into 6 pieces using template D (label these O) and 6 triangles using template C (label these P).

Green III:

Cut 1 strip 2¼″ × WOF; subcut into 15 triangles using template B (label these Q) and 15 triangles using template C (label these R).

Light green:

Cut 1 strip 2¼″ × WOF; subcut into 15 diamonds using template A. Label these S.

Cut 1 strip 2¼″ × WOF; subcut into 30 triangles using template B. Label these T.

Cut 1 strip 2¼″ × WOF; subcut into 30 triangles using template C. Label these U.

White I:

Cut 2 strips 2¼″ × WOF; subcut into 12 pieces using template D (label these V) and 12 triangles using template C (label these W).

Cut 4 strips 2¼″ × WOF.

White II:

Cut 3 strips 2¼″ × WOF; subcut into 18 pieces using template D (label these X) and 18 triangles using template C (label these Y).

White III:

Cut 1 strip 2¼″ × WOF; subcut into 30 triangles using template B. Label these Z.

Cut 1 strip 2¼″ × WOF; subcut into 30 triangles using template C. Label these AA.

Cream:

Cut 5 strips 4″ × WOF; subcut into 72 triangles [4″] using template E.

Cut 2 strips 2¼″ × WOF; subcut into 18 diamonds using template A. Label these BB.

Cut 1 strip 2¼″ × WOF; subcut into 30 triangles using template B. Label these CC.

Cut 1 strip 2¼″ × WOF; subcut into 30 triangles using template C. Label these DD.

WOF = width of fabric

Making the Triangles

Two pieced triangle designs—the star point and the star center triangles—make up the stars in the quilt. Each of the designs contains dark-value, light-value, and 1 of the 2 medium-value fabrics.

MAKING THE STAR POINT TRIANGLES

Star point triangle

There are 6 different colorways for the star point triangles. To make these large triangles, arrange the pieces as indicated by the letters in the diagrams and sew them together. Press. Make the required number of triangles for each colorway and label each with the star point number shown.

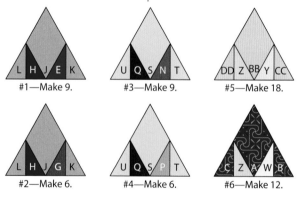

L H J E K
#1—Make 9.

U Q S N T
#3—Make 9.

DD Z BB Y CC
#5—Make 18.

L H J G K
#2—Make 6.

U Q S P T
#4—Make 6.

C Z A W B
#6—Make 12.

Make and label as shown.

MAKING THE STAR CENTER TRIANGLES

Star center triangle

There are 7 different colorways for the star center triangles. To make these large triangles, arrange the pieces as indicated by the letters in the diagrams and sew them together. Press. Make the required number of triangles for each colorway and label each with the star center number shown.

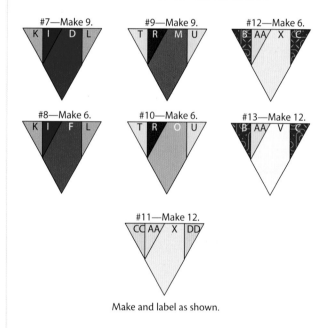

#7—Make 9.
K I D L

#9—Make 9.
T R M U

#12—Make 6.
B AA X C

#8—Make 6.
K I F L

#10—Make 6.
T R O U

#13—Make 12.
B AA V C

#11—Make 12.
CC AA X DD

Make and label as shown.

Assembling the Quilt Top

1. Arrange the star point and star center triangles in rows according to the numbers indicated in the quilt layout diagram, adding the cream background and border triangles where indicated. Sew the triangles into rows and press seams in alternate directions from row to row. Then sew the rows together.

Quilt layout

2. Refer to Appliqué (page 13) to prepare the small star appliqué, using the star template (page 80). Cut the star appliqué from white III fabric. Fuse the star to the quilt center (refer to the project photo, page 43, for placement), and stitch the raw edges with a small zigzag stitch.

3. Use your favorite methods to layer, quilt, and bind with the 2¼″ strips. I used silver thread to quilt the leaf designs on the stars; it adds extra sparkle. The background is quilted in a grid, and the star backgrounds are done with a free-motion pattern.

Quilting detail

LIFE LESSONS

by Coleen Barnhart
(the author's sister)

I went to a small church school for my first three years of grade school. When Valentine's Day drew near, my sisters and I would make valentines out of colored paper and lace doilies to give to our classmates. I envied those classmates who brought store-bought valentines to pass out. One year Mother made valentines for us to give to our friends by cutting out heart shapes on heavy paper. Then she placed three large candy hearts (the kind with sentiments on them) on the paper. She covered it with clear plastic and zigzagged around it with her Brother sewing machine. Our classmates loved those valentines. Another time Mother showed us how to weave little valentine baskets from construction paper to put candy in.

As I grew older, I realized that the homemade valentines were so much more special than the purchased ones. Things that involve a labor of love are more meaningful than things that are easily bought. Even if you don't have a lot of money, you can show your love by the effort you put into something.

STAR SHUFFLE

Made and machine quilted by Barbara Cline

Finished size: 52″ × 55″

The stars in this design are made with four values of six different colors. The nylon netting over half of each star diamond in this quilt creates the illusion that some star points are advancing forward and others are receding. When arranging the stars, it is important to keep enough contrast between the stars so they show up individually. This will take some moving around and changing of the pieces while working on the star layout. Notice that the placement of the graduated values also creates little stars within the big stars.

Materials

Yardage is based on 42"-wide fabric.

FOR STARS, ⅜ YARD EACH:

▦ **Brick red:** 4 values (1 dark, 1 medium, 1 medium-light, 1 light)

▦ **Blue:** 4 values (1 dark, 1 medium, 1 medium-light, 1 light)

▦ **Purple:** 4 values (1 dark, 1 medium, 1 medium-light, 1 light)

▦ **Green:** 4 values (1 dark, 1 medium, 1 medium-light, 1 light)

▦ **Burgundy:** 4 values (1 dark, 1 medium, 1 medium-light, 1 light)

▦ **Tan:** 4 values (1 dark, 1 medium,* 1 medium-light,* 1 light)

OTHER:

▦ **Brown print:** 1¾ yards for outside border and binding

▦ **Black nylon netting**: 108"-wide, ⅞ yard for overlays

▦ **Backing fabric:** 3¼ yards

▦ **Batting:** 58" × 61"

▦ **Template plastic**

▦ ***Plus** ¾ yard of medium tan for the second border and ¾ yard of medium-light tan for the background and borders

Cutting

Copy Star Shuffle templates A, B, and C (page 81) at 100%. Refer to Using Templates (page 7).

All brick red, blue, purple, and tan fabrics:

▦ Cut 4 strips 1½" × WOF.*

All green and burgundy fabrics:

▦ Cut 3 strips 1½" × WOF.

Medium-light tan:

▦ Cut 2 strips 1½" × WOF.

▦ Cut 2 strips 2⅞" × WOF; subcut into 10 triangles using template C.

▦ Cut 3 strips 3" × WOF.

Medium tan:

▦ Cut 6 strips 2" × WOF.

Brown print fabric:

▦ Cut 4 strips 3¾" × LOF.*

▦ From remaining fabric cut 230" of 2¼"-wide bias binding strips.

Netting:

▦ Cut 3 strips 9½" × WOF; subcut into 88 pieces 3½" × 9½".

*WOF = width of fabric; LOF = length of fabric

Making the Stars

To make the stars, you will pair strip-pieced triangles and sew them together using Y-seams to form larger 60° triangle units. On the sides of the quilt center, the light tan background triangles will form part of the triangle units.

MAKING THE STAR POINT DIAMONDS

For the diamond units, you will make strip sets from each of the colors, each graduating from the lightest to the darkest value. You will cut triangles from these strip sets, and the triangles will form diamonds in the quilt layout when the rows are sewn together. These are not sewn together yet, but are paired together for the layout to make sure you have the right number of cut pieces.

1. Arrange the strips of each colorway to form a strip set as shown without offsetting the strips. Stitch scant ¼" seams, and press the seams toward the dark fabrics. Make the following: 4 brick red strip sets, 4 blue strip sets, 4 purple strip sets, and 4 tan strip sets. Make 3 green strip sets and 3 burgundy strip sets.

| Dark |
| Medium |
| Medium-Light |
| Light |

Strip set

2. Use 2 strip sets each of the brick red, blue, purple, and tan to cut A pieces, tilting to the right. Position template A so that the lines on the template correspond with the seamlines of the strip sets. Rotate the template and cut another shape as you move along the strip. From the 2 strips you will cut 12 A triangles with light tips and 12 A triangles with dark tips. Put these into groups, labeling them "A (light tips)" and "A (dark tips)."

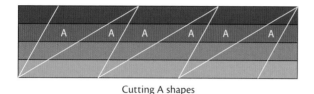

Cutting A shapes

3. Use 1½ strip sets each of the green and burgundy to cut A pieces as in Step 2. From the strips you will cut 8 A triangles with light tips and 8 A triangles with dark tips. Put these into groups, labeling them "A (light tips)" and "A (dark tips)."

4. Use 2 strip sets each of the brick red, blue, purple, and tan to cut B pieces, tilting to the left. Position template B so that the lines on the template correspond with the seamlines of the strip sets. Rotate the template and cut another shape as you move along the strip. From the 2 strips you will cut 12 B triangles with light tips and 12 B triangles with dark tips. Put these into groups, labeling them "B (light tips)" and "B (dark tips)."

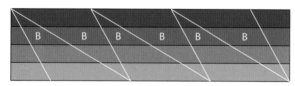

Cutting B shapes

5. Use 1½ strip sets each of the green and burgundy to cut B pieces as in Step 4. From the strips you will cut 8 B triangles with light tips and 8 B triangles with dark tips. Put these into groups, labeling them "B (light tips)" and "B (dark tips)."

6. Pair up A (light tips) with B (light tips) to make dark diamonds. Pair up A (dark tips) with B (dark tips) to make light diamonds as shown. Do *not* sew these together. Keep the A and B labels on the triangles. You will have extra triangles remaining for another project.

Dark diamond =   Light diamond =
A (light tip) + B (light tip)   A (dark tip) + B (dark tip)

Make the following pairs:

▥ **Brick red:** 10 dark diamonds and 5 light diamonds

▥ **Green:** 5 dark diamonds and 8 light diamonds

▥ **Tan:** 10 dark diamonds and 5 light diamonds

▥ **Blue:** 9 dark diamonds and 8 light diamonds

▥ **Purple:** 9 dark diamonds and 8 light diamonds

▥ **Burgundy:** 6 dark diamonds and 5 light diamonds

7. Refer to Overlays (page 14) and use the netting pieces as overlays on all the A pieces that you have put into pairs for the diamonds. Then pair them again with their mates.

Netting over left half of diamond darkens values.

8. Refer to the quilt layout diagram to arrange all the diamond pairs into stars. Arrange the background triangles along the sides of the quilt as shown in the diagram.

CONSTRUCTING THE TRIANGLE UNITS

Refer to Y-seams (page 12) for general instructions, and make the triangle units as indicated in the quilt layout diagram. Press the seams *open*. (Because there are 12 points coming together, this will help reduce the bulk in the seams.) Sew the triangle pairs into diamonds at the top and bottom of the quilt center. These will be completed with a border treatment later. Return all the units to the layout.

Assembling the Quilt Top

Refer to the quilt layout diagram to sew the triangle units into rows and sew together the rows. Press the seams open.

Quilt layout

 tip

Piece 2 triangle units at a time and then place the units in position. This will prevent you from getting all mixed up with the design placement.

ATTACHING THE BORDERS

Make 2 copies of Star Shuffle template D/E (page 82) at 200%. Refer to Using Templates (page 7).

The first side borders are medium-light tan strips, and the second side borders are medium tan strips. The top and bottom borders behind the stars are cut from medium-light tan / medium tan strip sets.

1. Sew the medium-light tan 1½″ side border strips to the sides of the quilt. Measure the length of the quilt through the center to calculate the lengths of the borders. Press the seams toward the border.

2. To make the top and bottom borders, sew together 3 medium tan 2″ strips end to end.

3. Sew together 3 medium-light tan 3″ strips end to end.

4. Sew these strips together lengthwise to make a long strip set. Press the seams toward the darker fabric.

5. From this strip, cut 4 trapezoids as shown, using template D.

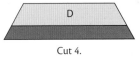

Cut 4.

6. For the border corners, cut 2 trapezoids using template E. Flip the template and cut 2 trapezoids using Er.

Cut 2 of each.

7. Refer to the quilt layout diagram for placement of the trapezoids and partial trapezoids between the star points and the corners. Sew these together using Y-seams. Press.

8. To add the side second borders, sew together the 3 medium tan 2″ strips end to end. Measure the length of the quilt through the center to calculate the lengths of the borders. Cut 2 border strips to this measurement from the long strip. Sew the strips to the sides of the quilt top. Press.

9. Refer to Mitered Borders (page 14) to add the outside border, using the brown print strips.

10. Use your favorite methods to layer, quilt, and bind the quilt with the 2¼" strips.. In the outside border, I quilted diamonds that connected tip to tip with a straight stitch. Next I quilted another row of diamonds, again connected tip to tip, with a serpentine stitch that offset the first row of diamonds. Then I quilted another row of diamonds with a zigzag stitch that offset the first and second rows of diamonds. Inside the quilt I stitched in-the-ditch.

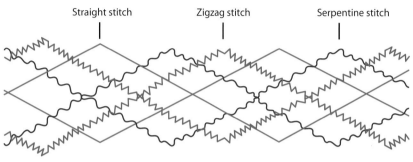

Straight stitch   Zigzag stitch   Serpentine stitch

Diagram of border quilting

Quilting detail

LIFE LESSONS

by Julia Graber
(the author's sister)

When I was around thirteen or fourteen, my mother gave me sewing lessons, which consisted of making a dress, step by step. I thought I could bypass the learning process and do it all on my own. Inevitably I would sew something wrong and have to pick out seams and redo them. Often tears of frustration would flow. But was I willing to back down and let Mother help me make the job easier? No! I was too full of myself to accept her love and help. My dear mother continued to love me in spite of myself and patiently pointed me in the right direction. I look back on that time with shame, but I am so grateful for a mother who did not give up on me. Today sewing is one of my great delights!

TRIANGLES TO DAISIES

Ring around the Posies, 47″ × 53″,
made and machine quilted by Barbara Cline

Whoever would have thought you could make a triangle into a daisy? One day I was playing on EQ and saw that I could turn a triangle into a daisy by shaping the end of the triangle into a heart-shaped curve and joining several of these pieces. The only problem was translating the design into a sewing method that worked. I tried piecing them to make a triangle, but this just would not work. But I kept on trying. A few days later that I tried appliqué—that worked! The results are lively quilts such as **Ring around the Posies**, *which uses the same pattern as* **Dazzling Daisies** *(page 54), and* **My Flower Garden** *(page 59).*

DAZZLING DAISIES

Made and machine quilted by Barbara Cline

Finished size: 47″ × 53″

Can you find the triangles in this quilt? They are the foundation onto which heart shapes have been appliquéd. Color values play an important part in this quilt. When I was working on it, I needed another color value to give the daisies some zip. That is when the nylon netting came into play. Placing an overlay over half of each heart shape creates another fabric color without picking two fabrics for each daisy. I used 19 different print fabrics for the daisies. You could use three colors of daisies and never have daisies of the same color next to each other.

After all the pieces are cut out, you will need an area large enough to lay out the complete quilt.

Materials

Yardage is based on 42"-wide fabric.

- **Reds:** 7 different fat quarters for daisies

- **Greens:** 6 different fat quarters for daisies

- **Blues:** 6 different fat quarters for daisies

- **Blue:** ⅜ yard for inside border (I matched one of the blue fat quarters.)

- **Rosy red:** 1⅝ yards for outside border and binding

- **Background fabric:** 1⅝ yards

- **Backing fabric:** 3 yards

- **Batting:** 53" × 59"

- **Batiste:** 1 yard for appliqué triangle foundations

- **Black nylon netting:** 108"-wide, ¾ yard

- **Double-sided fusible web:** 20"-wide, 5 yards

- **Template plastic**

- **Creative Grids 60° Triangle ruler** (optional)

Cutting

Copy Dazzling Daisies templates A and B (page 82) at 200%. Copy Dazzling Daisies template C (page 82) at 100%. Refer to Using Templates (page 7). [Optional: Refer to Using the Creative Grids 60° Triangle ruler (page 8) to cut the pieces with the ruler where the measurements are given in brackets.]

Background fabric:

- Cut 5 strips 7" × WOF;* subcut into 30 triangles [7"] using template A.

- Cut 1 strip 12" × WOF; subcut into 2 rectangles 12" × 20¾", position these with right sides together, and cut once diagonally.

Blue:

- Cut 6 strips 1½" × WOF.

Rosy red:

- Cut 4 strips 3½" × LOF.*

From remaining fabric, cut 215" of 2¼"-wide bias binding strips.

Batiste:

- Cut 4 strips 7" × WOF; subcut into 24 triangles [7"] using template A.

Nylon netting:

- Cut 3 strips 7¾" × WOF; subcut into 54 triangles [7¾"] using template B.

WOF = width of fabric; LOF = length of fabric

Preparing the Appliqués

1. Refer to Appliqué (page 13) to prepare the appliqués, tracing template C onto the fusible web. Make 114 pieces.

2. Roughly cut the pieces apart. Peel the paper off one side of the fusible web and fuse 6 shapes on the wrong side of each of the 19 different daisy fat quarters. Assign each fabric a number and label the appliqués with a number. For example, the reds will be R1, R2, and so on. Greens will be G1, G2, and so on. Blues will be B1, B2, and so on.

3. Cut out the heart shapes on the lines.

Making the Triangle Units

The heart-shaped "flower petals" are appliquéd onto triangles, and 6 triangle points come together in the center to form a daisy. The triangle units that make up the center daisies (center units) have 3 heart shapes, and the ones at the edges of the daisy cluster (edge units) have 1 or 2 heart shapes.

1. Each center unit will have 1 red, 1 green, and 1 blue appliqué, but each fabric appliqué will be in a unique position on the triangle, depending on the color reference numbers (R1, G2, and so on). No 2 center units are alike because of the variety of fabrics and the direction of the overlapping appliqués. Refer to the quilt layout diagram to place 3 hearts on a 7″ *batiste* triangle, noting the daisy color reference numbers and the direction of the overlaps. Fuse in place. Make a total of 24 unique center units.

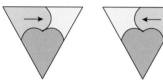

Variety of center units

2. For the edge units with 2 heart appliqués, each unit is unique (with no duplicates) because of the direction of the overlaps and variety of fabrics. Refer to the daisy center layout diagram to place 2 hearts on a 7″ *background* triangle, noting the daisy color reference numbers in the diagram and the direction of the overlaps for each triangle. Make a total of 12 unique 2-heart edge units.

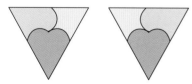

Edge units with 2 heart appliqués

3. For the edge units with 1 heart appliqué, there are some duplicates. The heart appliqués are again applied to 7″ background triangles. Refer to the daisy center layout diagram below with its fabric reference numbers to make 18 edge units with 1 heart appliqué.

Edge unit with 1 triangle

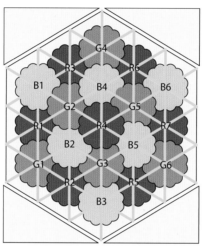

Daisy center layout

OVERLAYS AND APPLIQUÉS

Refer to Overlays (page 14). Using the netting triangles, you will apply overlays to the daisy triangle units. As you stitch the netting, you will be stitching around the appliqués that have been fused to the units. You will trim away the netting on the left side of each heart, leaving the netting overlay on the right side.

1. Place a 7¾″ piece of nylon netting over a daisy triangle unit. Pin it in position and use a small zigzag stitch to appliqué down the center and then around the curved edge of each heart. Refer to the numbers in the diagrams for the correct stitching order. (Experiment on some scraps to find the stitch setting you like for your machine.) Stitch the straight line on the heart first, and then the curved line.

 tip

> I changed thread color when appliquéing, which can be time consuming. If you use a variegated thread that blends with all the fabrics, there is no need to change thread colors.

Stitching order for 1 heart

Stitching order for 2 hearts

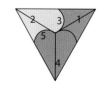

Stitching order for 3 hearts

2. Refer to the diagram to see where to trim the netting away. (Helpful hint: Position any triangle in front of you with the point toward you. On the heart appliqué nearest you, trim away the netting on the left side of the heart. The netting on the right side of the heart remains. Rotate the triangle so the next point is facing you, and again trim away the netting on the left side of that heart appliqué. Continue rotating the triangle to trim away the netting as needed.)

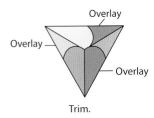

 tip

As you hold the scissors, turn your palm up so the scissor blades are almost flat against the fabric, and then slip the tip of your scissors between the netting and the fabric. This will keep you from cutting the fabric underneath the netting. Use small, sharp scissors so you can trim close to the lines of stitching.

Assembling the Quilt Top

1. Sew the triangles into rows as shown in the quilt layout diagram. Press the seams open. Add the large background triangles to each corner. Press the seams toward the background triangles. If needed, square up the quilt top after adding the large triangles.

2. Refer to Mitered Borders (page 14) and use the blue 1½″ strips and the rosy red 3½″ strips to make the border.

Quilt layout

3. Use your favorite methods to layer, quilt, and bind the quilt with the 2¼″ strips. I used variegated thread and a small zigzag stitch to create curlicue designs in the light-colored daisy petals and simple patterns in the darker petals.

Detail of quilting

Detail from *Ring around the Posies* (page 53)

This variation has a brighter color scheme of pinks and greens with black accents. When it came time to quilt this, I wanted to emphasize the daisy design. I quilted a design on each daisy that echoed the pieced shapes, and I also quilted the daisy design in green thread on the white background.

Detail of quilting

LIFE LESSONS

by Sheila Helmuth
(the author's sister)

Sewing and piecing have never been my cup of tea, but over the past several years as I have watched my mother, sisters, and nieces work with their hands and create beautiful quilts, comforters, dresses, and other works of art, my interest has grown. At first, I felt like I did not have the patience or even enough interest to make a project. I thought I probably wouldn't be able to figure it out if I did start! But my sisters continually encouraged me to try it out, offering all kinds of help and support, and eventually I took them up on it. So now, every year when we sisters have our annual weeklong sewing retreat, I bring my two or three projects along, knowing that if I get stuck, someone in the group will be more than willing to get me back on track. Currently, I have completed two comforters, and I have one quilt top pieced that is now ready for quilting. My current project is a velvet comforter, which I am looking forward to finishing one of these days … but I'm in no hurry. I know that with help and encouragement, I can do it!

Pieced by Barbara Cline and quilted by Margaret Wade

Finished size: 85" × 104"

In this design, daisies are centered in stars on hexagon backgrounds, so the quilt design looks complex. But it is made with simple strip piecing and appliqué. The hexagons behind the stars are made using strip sets. You will be able to make light-to-dark and dark-to-light background units from the same strip sets, so there will be very little waste. The light-to-dark values of the daisies and the hexagons, accented with black, make a bright, lively pattern. I used a great variety of fabrics for the petals of my flowers, but I have simplified these instructions by using only twelve fabrics in the flowers—still plenty of variety.

Materials

Yardage is based on 42"-wide fabric.

▪ **Red:** 1 yard each of 4 values (light, medium-light, medium, dark)

▪ **Green:** 1 yard each of 4 values (light, medium-light, medium, dark)

▪ **Yellow:** 1 yard each of 4 values (light, medium-light, medium, dark)

▪ **Border print:** 3⅜ yards

▪ **Solid black:** 3¼ yards for stars, background, and first top and bottom borders

▪ **Black print:** 2½ yards for stars

▪ **Binding:** ¾ yard

▪ **Backing fabric:** 7¾ yards

▪ **Batting:** 93" × 112"

▪ **Double-sided fusible web:** 20" wide, 2⅛ yards

▪ **Creative Grids 60° Triangle ruler** (optional)

▪ **Template plastic**

Cutting

Copy My Flower Garden templates A–D (pages 83 and 84) at 100%. Refer to Using Templates (page 7). [Optional: Refer to Using the Creative Grids 60° Triangle ruler (page 8) to cut the pieces with the ruler; use the measurements given in brackets.]

All reds (light, medium-light, medium, and dark):

▪ Cut 8 strips 1¾" × WOF.*

▪ Cut 3 strips 3½" × WOF; subcut into 18 rectangles 3½" × 6¼".

All greens (light, medium-light, medium, and dark):

▪ Cut 8 strips 1¾" × WOF.

▪ Cut 3 strips 3½" × WOF; subcut into 18 rectangles 3½" × 6¼".

All yellows (light, medium-light, medium, and dark):

▪ Cut 8 strips 1¾" × WOF.

▪ Cut 3 strips 3½" × WOF; subcut into 18 rectangles 3½" × 6¼".

Border print:

▪ Cut 4 strips 5¾" × length of fabric.

Solid black:

▪ Cut 22 strips 3½" × WOF; subcut into 108 pieces using template A.

▪ Cut 2 strips 11" × WOF; subcut into 9 rectangles 6½" × 11"; then, with fabric facing up, cut diagonally from the upper left to the lower right corners to make 18 triangles.

▪ Cut 4 strips 2" × WOF for the first top and bottom borders.

Black print:

▪ Cut 22 strips 3½" × WOF; subcut into 108 pieces using template A.

Binding:

▪ Cut 10 strips 2¼" × WOF.

Double-sided fusible web:

▪ Cut 216 rectangles 2" × 3".

WOF = width of fabric

Making the Triangles

The triangles will form part of the hexagon units and are cut from strip sets. Refer to Cutting from Strip Sets (page 10). You will make 36 A triangles (dark red on the bottom) and 36 B triangles (light red on the bottom).

1. To make a strip set, place a light red 1¾″ strip on your cutting mat, and below it place a medium-light red 1¾″ strip, then a medium red 1¾″ strip, and finally a dark red 1¾″ strip. These strips are not offset from row to row. Sew the strips together lengthwise with scant ¼″ seams, and then press the seams toward the darker fabrics. Make 8 strip sets each of reds, greens, and yellows.

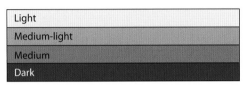

| Light |
| Medium-light |
| Medium |
| Dark |

Make 8 sets of each color group.

2. Use template D to cut triangles [5½″] from the strip sets. Rotate the template [ruler] and cut another triangle. Continue along the strip sets to cut 72 triangles from each color—36 A triangles and 36 B triangles.

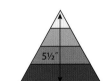

Cut 36 A triangles each of red, green, and yellow.

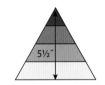

Cut 36 B triangles each of red, green, and yellow.

Making the Daisy Petals

You will need 2 different petals—B and C—for each daisy in the quilt. Refer to Appliqué (page 13) for general instructions.

1. To make the daisy petals, follow the manufacturer's instruction for the fusible web and fuse a 2″ × 3″ rectangle to the fabric back at one end of every 3½″ × 6¼″ piece as shown.

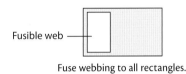

Fusible web

Fuse webbing to all rectangles.

2. From the right side of the fabric, position the petal template B on a light red rectangle with the curved end of the template over the fused area of the rectangle as shown. Make sure that the entire curved area is within the fused area. Trace around the template and then cut out the appliqué. Cut 18 B petals of light red, medium-light red, light green, medium-light green, light yellow, and medium-light yellow. You will have 108 B petals.

Daisy petal B

3. Using petal template C in the same manner (curved end of the template is over the fused area), trace and cut out 18 C petals from medium red, dark red, medium green, dark green, medium yellow, and dark yellow. You will have 108 C petals.

Daisy petal C

Making the Diamond Units

The diamond petal units will form the stars in the quilt top. You will make 18 diamonds of each petal color combination.

1. To form a diamond, lay out a black print piece A and a solid black piece A together as shown, with the print piece on the left and higher than the solid black piece. Do not join these yet.

Diamond

2. Remove the paper backing from a light red B petal, and place it on the print piece A as shown. Remove the paper from a medium C petal and place it on the black solid fabric as shown. Line up the bottom edges and fuse the petals in place.

Two half-diamonds

3. Pin together the 2 half-diamonds and sew. Press the seam open.

4. Refer to Appliqué (page 13) to stitch the curved edges of the appliqués.

5. Repeat Steps 1–4 to make the following:

- 18 units with light red petal B on black print A and medium red petal C on black solid A

- 18 units with medium-light red petal B on black print A and dark red petal C on black solid A

- 18 units with light green petal B on black print A and medium green petal C on black solid A

- 18 units with medium-light green petal B on black print A and dark green petal C on black solid A

- 18 units with light yellow petal B on black print A and medium yellow petal C on black solid A

- 18 units with medium-light yellow petal B on black print A and dark yellow petal C on black solid A

Making the Triangle Units

When arranged in the quilt layout, these large triangle units will form the stars. You'll make 18 triangle units of each color.

1. Sew 36 red A triangles to 18 light red / medium red diamonds as shown. Make 18.

Triangle A added to each side

2. Sew 36 red B triangles to 18 medium-light red / dark red diamonds as shown. Make 18.

Triangle B added to each side

3. Repeat Steps 1 and 2 with the greens and yellows.

Assembling the Quilt Top

1. Lay out the quilt top according to the quilt layout diagram. It is easiest to lay this out by placing a complete 6-piece set of hexagon triangle units first, then adding another complete hexagon, and so forth. Place the yellow half-hexagons at the top and bottom as shown. Then place the solid black background setting triangles along the sides of the quilt top.

2. Sew the triangles together in rows as shown and press the seams open. Sew together the rows and press.

3. Measure through the horizontal center of the quilt to determine the border length for the top and bottom of the quilt center. Using the black 2″ strips, cut 2 pieces to this measurement, joining the strips as necessary. Sew these to the top and bottom of the quilt. Press the seams toward the border.

4. Refer to Mitered Borders (page 14) to sew the 5¾″ borders to all sides of the quilt top.

5. Use your favorite methods to layer, quilt, and bind with the 2¼″ strips. Margaret quilted daisy petal designs on the hexagons and curved pinwheels on the daisies.

Quilt layout

Quilting detail

LIFE LESSONS

by Polly Yoder
(the author's sister)

A couple of years ago, a friend posted a quote on a blog site that made an impression on me and continues to influence how I respond to the many people who come into my life.

> *People may forget what you do—*
> *They may forget what you say—*
> *But they will never forget how you make them feel.*

I have thought of this saying from time to time and have resolved to be more in tune with how I make people feel. Above all else, I want my family and friends to feel my love, but I sometimes struggle with how to put into words what is in my heart. Because of this, I often demonstrate my love for them in more tangible ways. Since God has chosen to bless me with artistic ability and a love for piecing, what better way to make my family and friends feel loved than to wrap them up in comforters and quilts made by my own hands? These creations have become a legacy to my children, my grandchildren, and even my friends. These things say, "You're special, and I surely do love you!" They may forget things about me, and they may forget what I say, but my hope is that they will look at the tangible evidence of my love for them and remember that I love them so intensely that I stitched that love into a kaleidoscope of colors just for them.

Yes, it takes time. It takes energy, effort, practice, and a sense of balance and precision to make a quilt to my satisfaction—but for as long as I can, I plan to keep on sewing and stitching. I always want to wrap my loved ones in quilts that I've made—quilts made especially for them.

TRIANGLES TO PINWHEELS

Pinwheel Spin, 55" × 80",
made by Barbara Cline and Parla Sonifrank and
machine quilted by Barbara Cline

*You will have to look closely to find the triangles in these
pinwheel quilt designs. In both designs, the triangle is the
basic assembly unit as well as being used in subtle ways to
create the pinwheels. These quilts are surprisingly simple
to put together, and creative use of color and value makes
the most of the lively designs.*

BUTTON, BUTTON,
WHO'S GOT THE BUTTON?

Made and machine quilted by Barbara Cline

Finished size: 70″ × 61″

Look for the triangles in these pinwheel designs—they're subtle. The pinwheels are composed of diamonds and triangles made with a combination of light-value background fabrics and darker-value fabrics, so that the background areas "disappear" and reveal the darker pinwheel shapes. The small pinwheels are made up of pieced triangle units, and the large pinwheels are made with diamond units.

This quilt looks quite complicated, but after you piece the triangles, the quilt just flows together. Notice how four pinwheels are pieced in the hexagonal border. The bright, cheerful colors chosen for the pinwheels coordinate with the eye-catching striped border fabric. The buttons in the centers of the pinwheels give this quilt a special touch.

Materials

Yardage is based on 42"-wide fabric.

▨ **Fat quarters:** 7 in medium and dark values of yellow, green, red, red/brown, and orange for large and small pinwheels

▨ **Fat eighths:** 9 in medium and dark values of yellow, green, red, red/brown, and orange for small pinwheels

▨ **Background fabrics:** 8 in light yellows and creams, ⅝ yard of each

▨ **Striped fabric:** 1 yard for border

▨ **Black fabric:** ½ yard for binding

▨ **Backing fabric:** 3¾ yards

▨ **Batting:** 76" × 67"

▨ **Buttons:** 23 in 1"–1¼" diameters

▨ **Template plastic**

Cutting

Copy Button, Button templates A–E (pages 84 and 85) at 100%. Refer to Using Templates (page 7).

Each fat quarter:

▨ Cut 2 strips 3" × 21"; subcut into 6 pieces using template D for a total of 42.

▨ Cut 2 strips 2⅜" × 21"; subcut into 6 pieces using template C for a total of 42.

Each fat eighth:

▨ Cut 2 strips 2⅜" × 21"; subcut into 6 pieces using template C for a total of 54.

Each background fabric:

▨ Cut 1 strip 3⅛" × WOF;* subcut into 12 pieces using template A for a total of 96.

▨ Cut 1 strip 2⅞" × WOF; subcut into 12 pieces using template B for a total of 96.

▨ Cut 1 strip 3" × WOF from 7 of the fabrics; subcut into 6 pieces using template D for a total of 42.

▨ Cut 1 strip 4⅞" × WOF; subcut into 6 triangles using template E for a total of 48.

Striped fabric:

▨ Cut 6 strips 4⅞" × WOF.

Black fabric:

▨ Cut 6 strips 2¼" × WOF.

*WOF = width of fabric

Making the Small Pinwheel Triangle Units

1. Make a group with 6 A pieces, 6 B matching background fabric triangles, and 6 C triangles of the same color. To form one triangle unit, sew A to C and then add the B piece. Press the seams toward the darker fabric. Complete all 6 triangle units. Together this set makes 1 small pinwheel in the quilt layout.

Small pinwheel triangle unit

2. Complete 15 additional pinwheel sets by repeating Step 1. You'll need a total of 16 small pinwheel sets.

Making the Large Pinwheel Diamond Units

1. Make a group of 6 matching background D pieces and 6 matching color D pieces. Sew a background D piece and a color D piece together as shown. Press toward the darker fabric. Repeat to make a set of 6 diamonds. Together this set makes 1 large pinwheel in the quilt layout.

Diamond unit

2. Repeat Step 1 to complete a total of 7 sets of large pinwheel diamonds.

Preparing the Border Strips

1. Using only 2 of the 4⅞″ border strips, cut a 60° angle on the right end as shown. These are border strips 1 and 4.

60° cut

2. Using the remaining 4 border strips, cut a 60° angle on the left end as shown. These are border strips 2, 3, 5, and 6.

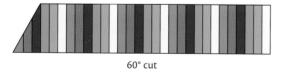

60° cut

3. Sew the small pinwheel units (with the blue outlines in the quilt layout diagram) to the angled ends of border strips 2, 3, 5, and 6.

Borders 2, 3, 5, and 6

Assembling the Quilt Top

1. Arrange the small triangle and diamond units to form the outlined triangles shown in the quilt layout diagram. You can see how 4 small triangle units form a large triangle (black outlines in the diagram) and 2 small triangle units with a large diamond also form large triangles (also black outlines). Sew each large triangle together, and replace it in the layout. Visually, you can see the hexagons of the small pinwheels emerge.

Quilt layout

2. Sew the large triangle units into rows. Press, and sew the rows together to create a large hexagon. Press.

ADDING THE BORDERS

1. Refer to the quilt layout diagram for the sewing order. Position border strip 1 so the angled right end is even with the quilt top edge and the left end extends beyond the quilt top. Begin sewing 15″ from the left end, leaving it free. Press the seams toward the border.

2. Position each of the borders in the same way as you sew on borders 2, 3, 4, 5, and 6. Press the seams toward the border. Then complete the seam on the first border.

3. Trim off the border ends as indicated by the black lines as shown in the quilt layout (page 68).

4. Use your favorite methods to layer, quilt, and bind with the 2¼″ strips. Sew buttons to the centers of each pinwheel.

For this quilt I quilted an allover stippling or meandering design in the background and quilted feathers in the pinwheels.

Quilting detail

LIFE LESSONS

by Emily Hostetler
(the author's sister)

I well remember how, when I was fifteen years old, my parents purchased a small rural fabric store to give my sisters and me work to do. We were all plunged into the world of fabric and business whether we liked it or not. I did like to create and sew projects, but I had no idea that this experience would provide me with opportunities later in life. I know there were many days when I thought the store was not worth the effort and did not enjoy going to work. But I now understand and value the way in which fabric stores encourage community, fellowship, and friendship. Now, more than ever, I value the time I am able to spend with my first daughter-in-law as we sew and go fabric shopping together. I only had sons, so I was never able to teach a daughter to sew; now I am enjoying the new opportunities I have with my daughter-in-law. One of my favorite words now is "sew-cialize." I have learned that the opportunities we have are more important than the ones we wish we had.

PINWHEEL SPIN

Pieced by Parla Sonifrank and Barbara Cline, and machine quilted by Barbara Cline

Finished size: 68″ × 91″

My daughter Parla and I made this quilt. We both picked the colors, and she did most of the cutting and pressing while I did most of the sewing. This quilt is a good one for using small amounts of fabric from your stash. Parla strategically arranged the pinwheels, starting at the top with greens, graduating to browns, and finishing with the blues at the bottom. In placing the pinwheels, it's important to make sure there is a value difference between pinwheels that are beside each other. Stand back about fifteen to twenty feet and squint your eyes. If the colors blend together, there is not enough contrast between the fabrics. It's fun to move the pinwheels around, to see which pinwheels complement each other and what pleases the eye.

Materials

Yardage is based on 42"-wide fabric.

- **Fabrics:** 45 varieties, ⅛ yard each, for pinwheels

- **Brown:** 4⅛ yards total (2¾ yards for background, 30° triangles, and borders; 1⅜ yards for pinwheels)

- **Green:** ¾ yard for second border

- **Binding fabric:** ¾ yard

- **Backing fabric:** 5½ yards

- **Batting:** 76" × 99"

- **Template plastic**

- **Creative Grids 60° Triangle ruler** (optional)

Cutting

Copy Pinwheel Spin templates A and B (page 86) at 100%. Refer to Using Templates (page 7) to cut the indicated triangles. [Optional: Refer to Using the Creative Grids 60° Ruler (page 8) to cut the triangles; use the measurements given in brackets.]

45 different fabrics:

- Cut 1 strip 3" × WOF;* subcut into 6 pieces using template A.

Brown (2¾ yards):

- Cut 4 strips 3½" × LOF.*

- Cut 4 strips 4½" × LOF.

- Cut 1 strip 7½" × LOF; subcut 7 triangles using template B and 7 triangles using template Br [7 sets of mirror-image 30° triangles 7½"].

Brown (1⅜ yards):

- Cut 15 strips 3" × WOF; subcut into 87 pieces using template A.

Green:

- Cut 8 strips 2½" × WOF.

Binding fabric:

- Cut 9 strips 2¼" × WOF.

*WOF = width of fabric; LOF = length of fabric

Quilt Layout

The blades of each pinwheel interlock with the blades of the next pinwheel, with no space between the designs. This continuous design pattern is called a tessellation. The challenge and the fun of this project are the layout—with 45 different fabrics creating 45 unique pinwheels. *The quilt must be completely laid out before any sewing is done.*

 tip

I like to lay my quilt pieces out on the back of a flannel-backed tablecloth. I make 1-foot folds across the tablecloth's width and then fold it into 4 sections in the other direction. This allows me to put it away until a later date for piecing. When ready to piece again, I unfold it carefully, and I'm all ready to start sewing.

1. Begin by choosing a pinwheel color. On your design surface, arrange 6 blades (A pieces) to create a pinwheel.

First pinwheel

2. To this pinwheel, add another pinwheel so that the blades interlock as shown.

Two interlocking pinwheels

3. Add another interlocking pinwheel as shown.

Third pinwheel

4. Continue adding pinwheels until the complete quilt top is laid out in offset rows of 3 pinwheels, as shown in the quilt layout diagram. Refer to the quilt layout diagram to add the brown blades (A pieces) to finish the triangle units along the quilt edges. Add the brown 30° triangles to the top and bottom of the quilt. Use 3 brown A pieces to form 2 brown triangles at the right edge near the top and bottom of the quilt.

Since this is a scrappy quilt, I like to change and rearrange the pinwheels to flow from color to color. Keep in mind that there should always be a color value difference between pinwheels that touch each other.

Constructing the Triangle Units

The A pieces form triangle units that you will sew together using Y-seams. When the triangles are joined together, the blades of the pinwheels interlock with each other across the quilt, creating the tessellation of pinwheels.

1. Refer to the quilt layout diagram again to identify the triangles formed with the A pieces. Sew each triangle unit together, following the instructions for Y-seams (page 12).

Triangle unit

2. Sew the triangles into vertical rows and press. Then sew the rows together. Press in alternate directions from row to row.

3. Sew the green strips end-to-end then, referring to Mitered Borders (page 14), use brown 4½" strips (first border), green 2½" strips (second border), and brown 3½" strips (third border) to finish the quilt top.

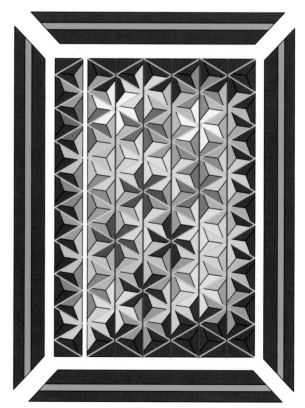

Quilt layout

4. Use your favorite methods to layer, quilt, and bind with the 2¼″ strips.

Here, you can see that I quilted different leaf motifs inside the pinwheels.

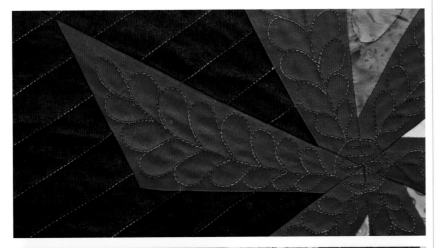

Quilting details

LIFE LESSONS

by Cheryl Heatwole
(the author's sister-in-law)

Nineteen years ago I decided to piece a Log Cabin quilt. I was so excited about it. It would match our bedroom, and I had chosen the latest and greatest colors. I worked on it here and there, but it was several years before I finally finished piecing the top. By the time I finished, I had two children, we had moved, and our bedroom was a different color. I no longer thought the colors were so late and great. So I packed it up and put it away, thinking I would eventually go back to it. All these years later, it is still folded up, unfinished. I have since completed other projects, and it is such a joy to use them while they are still colors that I enjoy looking at. Maybe someday the colors of that Log Cabin quilt will come back in and I will decide to finish it, but until then I'll avoid procrastinating so that I can finish my projects while I still love the patterns and colors that I chose.

Template Patterns

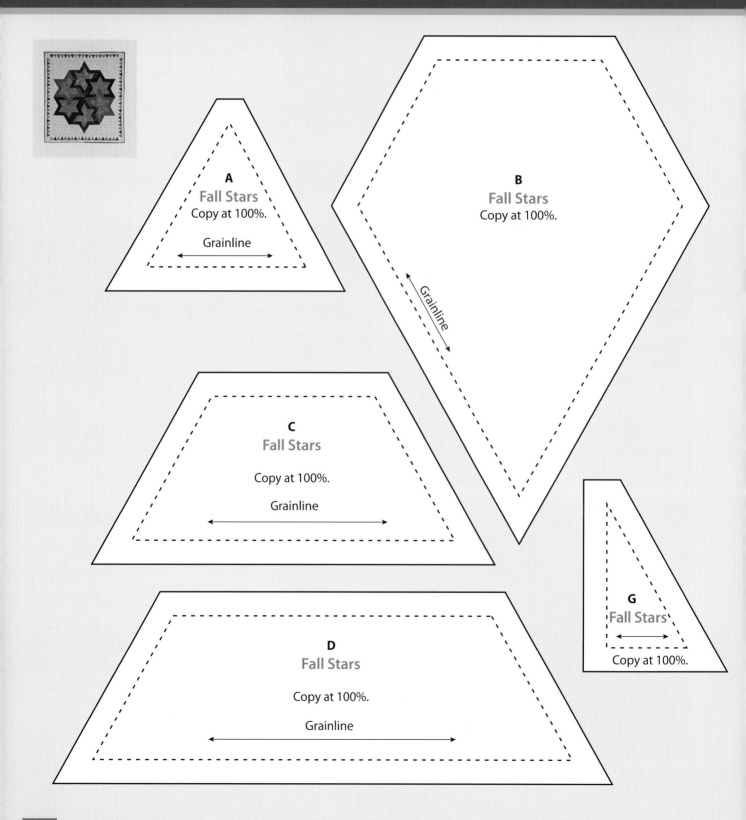

A
Fall Stars
Copy at 100%.

Grainline

B
Fall Stars
Copy at 100%.

Grainline

C
Fall Stars

Copy at 100%.

Grainline

G
Fall Stars

Copy at 100%.

D
Fall Stars

Copy at 100%.

Grainline

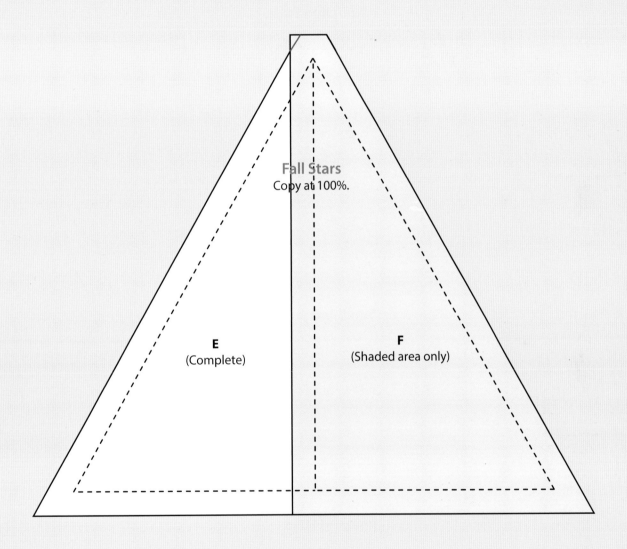

Fall Stars
Copy at 100%.

E
(Complete)

F
(Shaded area only)

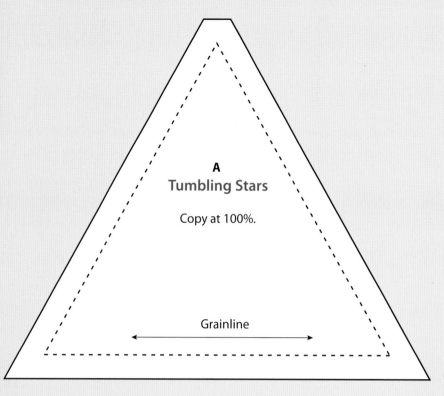

A
Tumbling Stars

Copy at 100%.

Grainline

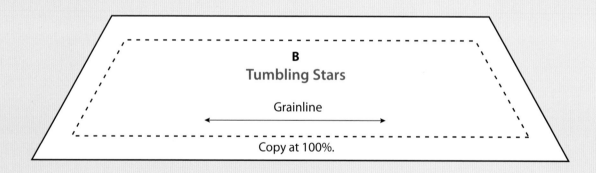

B
Tumbling Stars

Grainline

Copy at 100%.

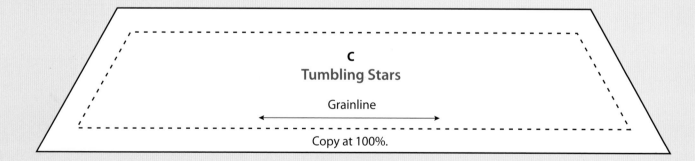

C
Tumbling Stars

Grainline

Copy at 100%.

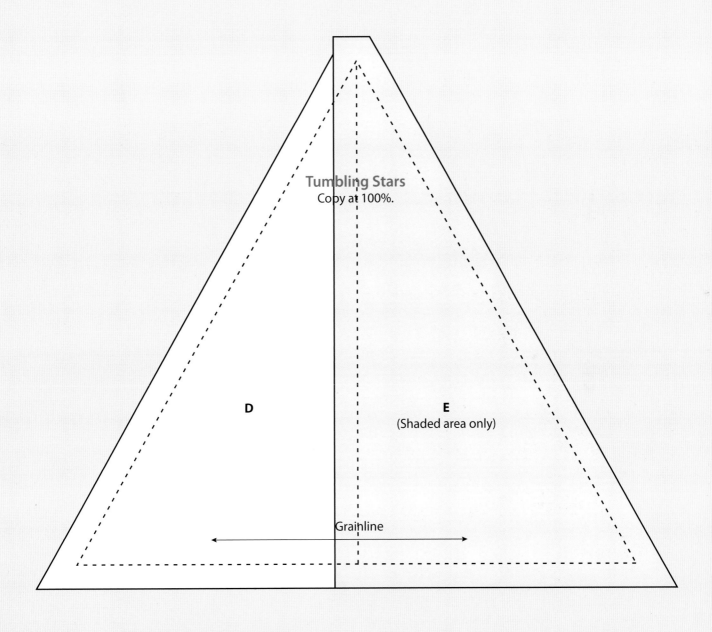

Tumbling Stars
Copy at 100%.

D

E
(Shaded area only)

Grainline

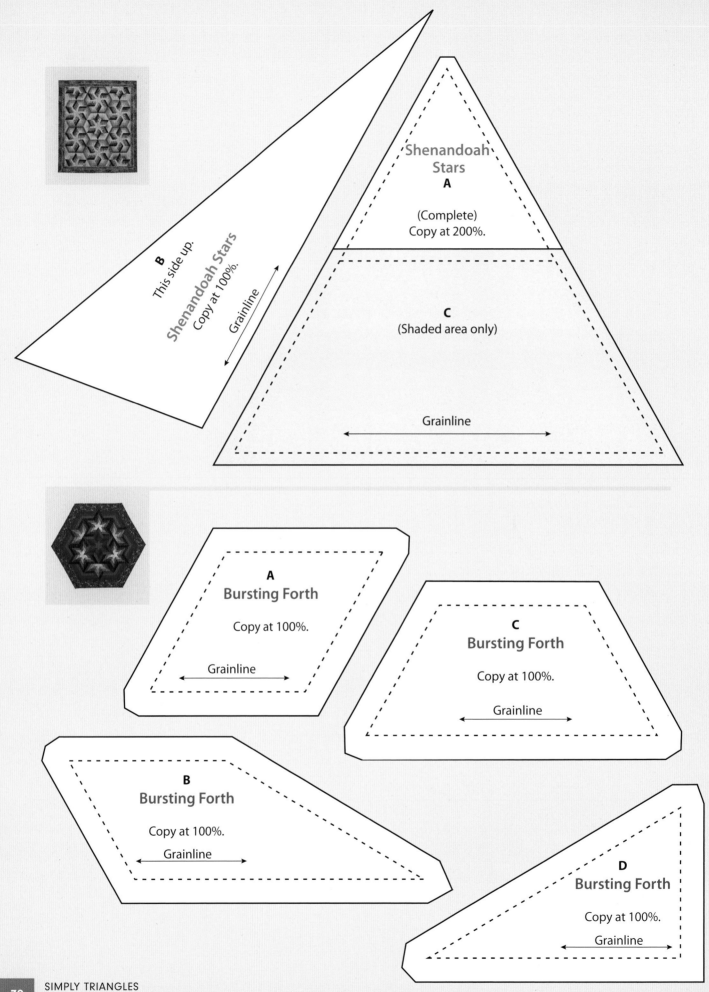

B
This side up.
Shenandoah Stars
Copy at 100%.
Grainline

Shenandoah Stars
A

(Complete)
Copy at 200%.

C
(Shaded area only)

Grainline

A
Bursting Forth

Copy at 100%.

Grainline

C
Bursting Forth

Copy at 100%.

Grainline

B
Bursting Forth

Copy at 100%.

Grainline

D
Bursting Forth

Copy at 100%.

Grainline

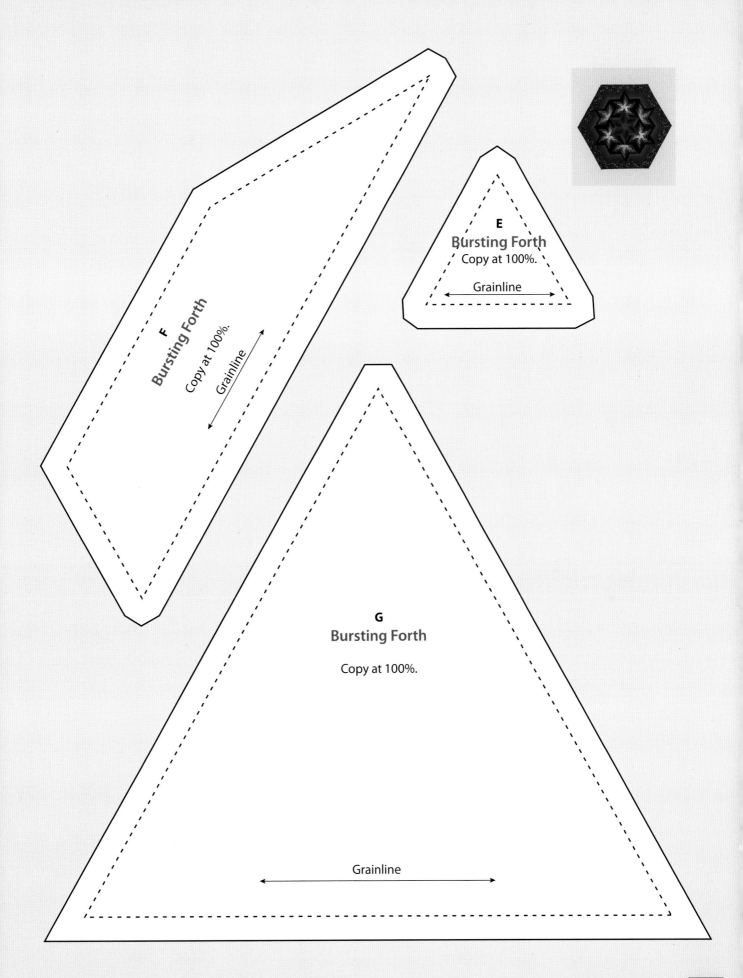

F
Bursting Forth
Copy at 100%.

Grainline

E
Bursting Forth
Copy at 100%.

Grainline

G
Bursting Forth

Copy at 100%.

Grainline

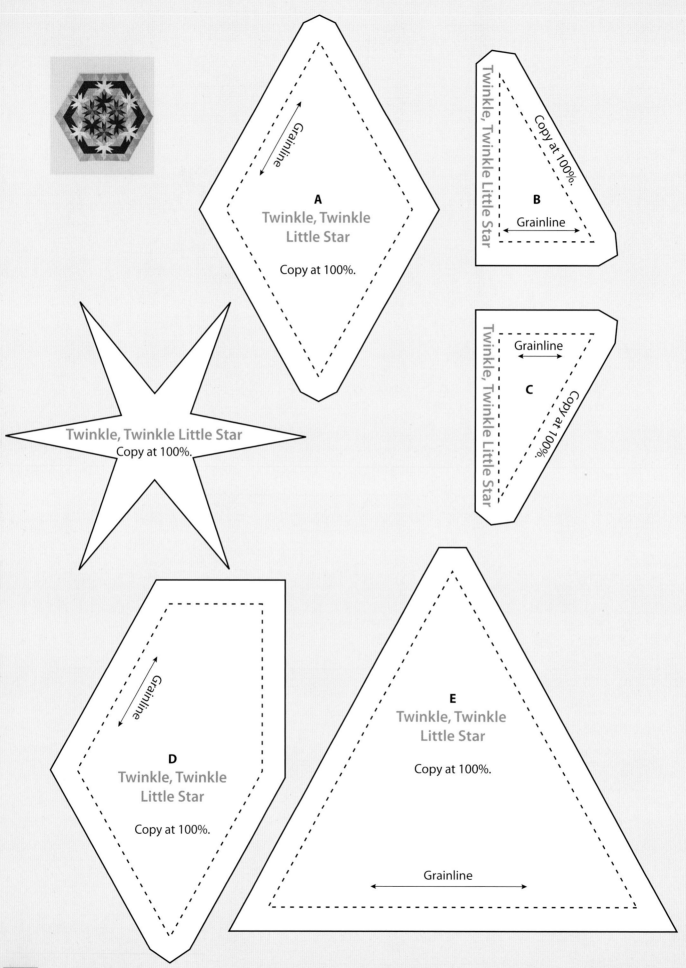

A
Twinkle, Twinkle
Little Star

Copy at 100%.

Grainline

Twinkle, Twinkle Little Star
Copy at 100%.

B
Copy at 100%.
Twinkle, Twinkle Little Star
Grainline

C
Copy at 100%.
Twinkle, Twinkle Little Star
Grainline

D
Twinkle, Twinkle
Little Star

Copy at 100%.

Grainline

E
Twinkle, Twinkle
Little Star

Copy at 100%.

Grainline

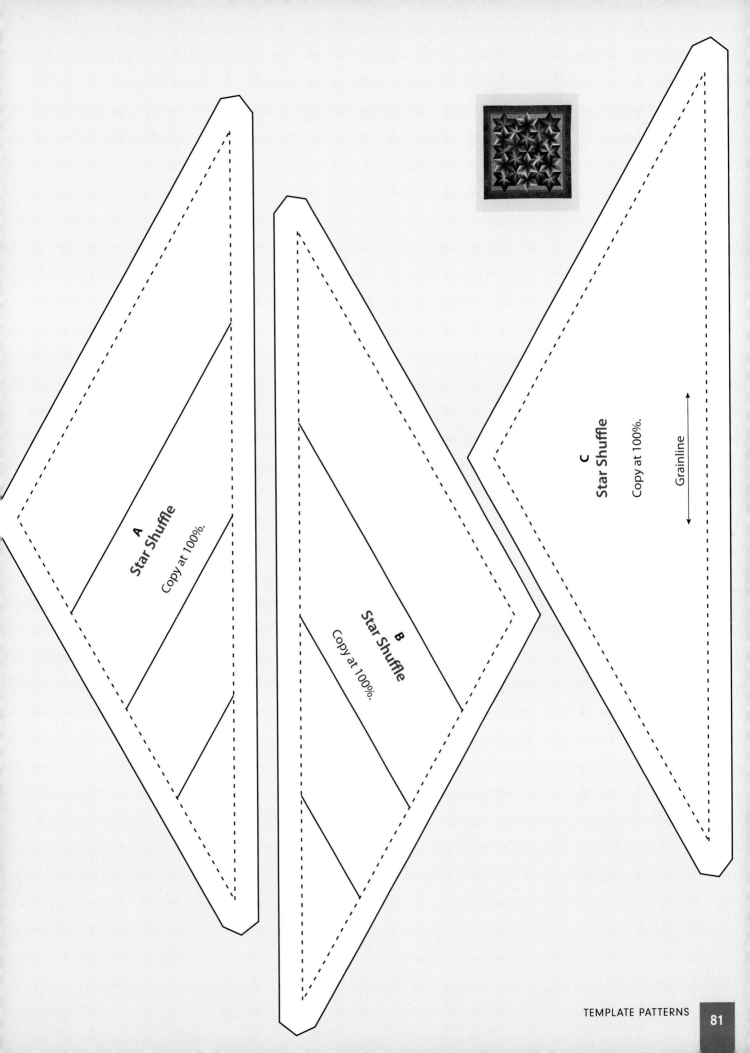

A
Star Shuffle
Copy at 100%.

B
Star Shuffle
Copy at 100%.

C
Star Shuffle
Copy at 100%.

Grainline

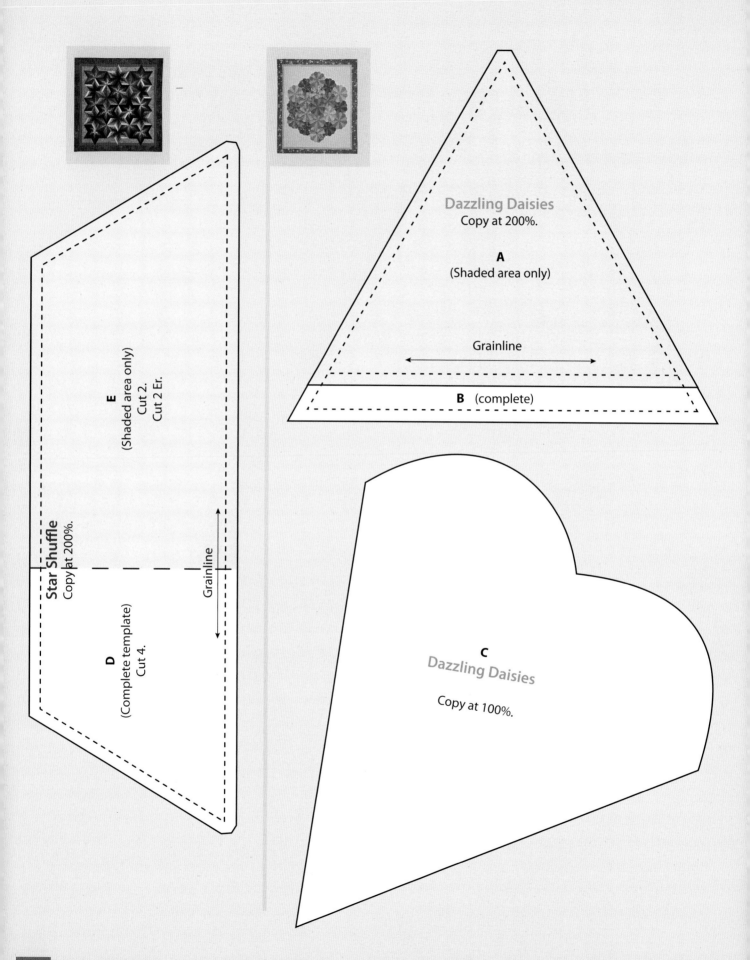

Dazzling Daisies
Copy at 200%.

A
(Shaded area only)

Grainline

B (complete)

E
(Shaded area only)
Cut 2.
Cut 2 Er.

Star Shuffle
Copy at 200%.

Grainline

D
(Complete template)
Cut 4.

C
Dazzling Daisies

Copy at 100%.

A

My Flower Garden

Copy at 100%.

Keep this side up.

Grainline

B

My Flower Garden

Copy at 100%.

Keep this side up.

C

My Flower Garden

Copy at 100%.

Keep this side up.

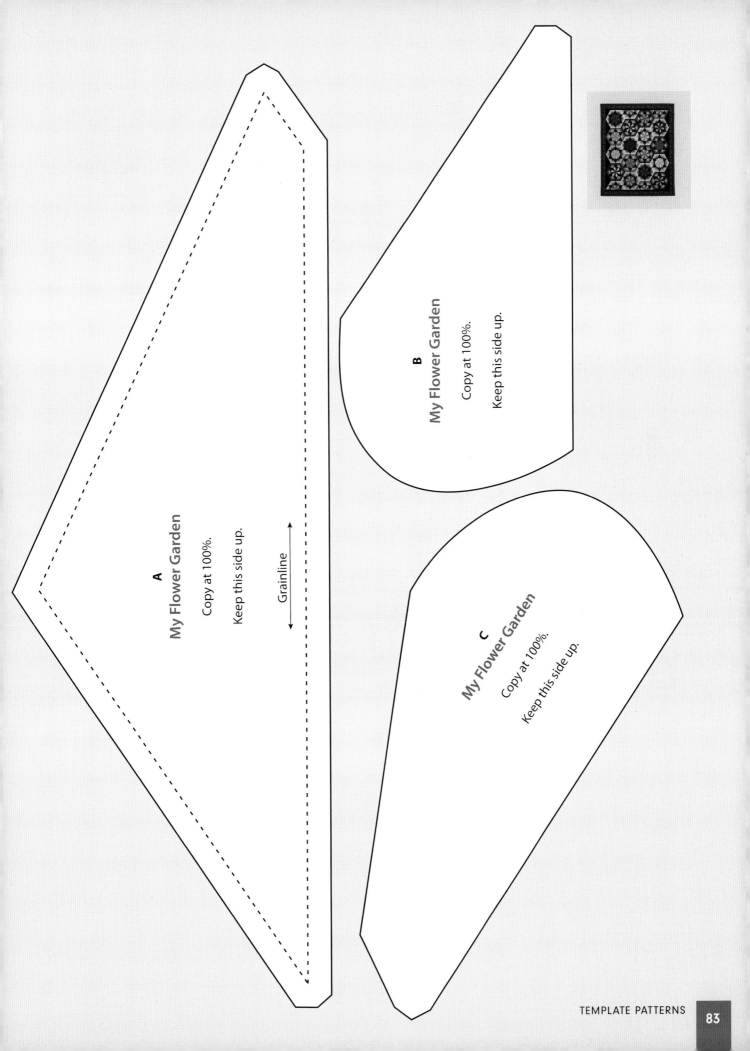

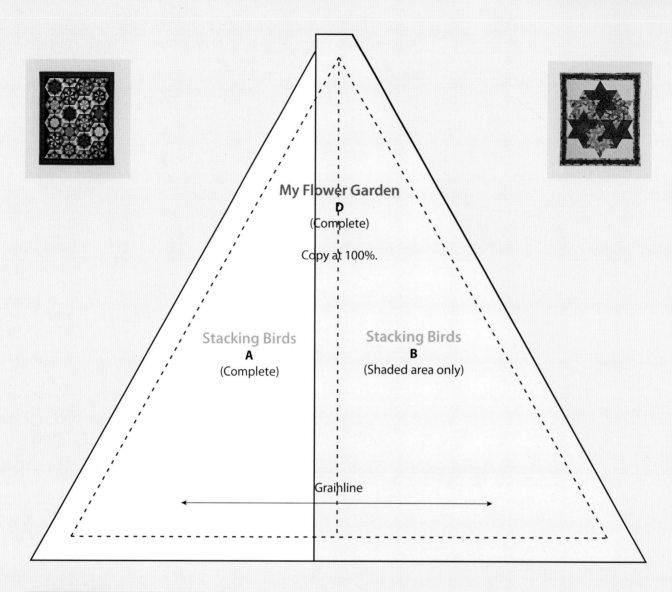

My Flower Garden
D
(Complete)

Copy at 100%.

Stacking Birds
A
(Complete)

Stacking Birds
B
(Shaded area only)

Grainline

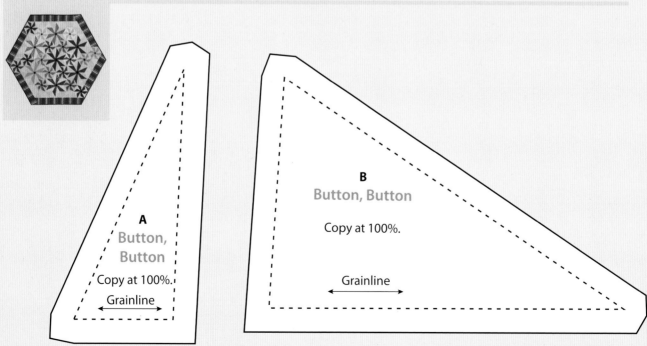

A
Button,
Button

Copy at 100%.

Grainline

B
Button, Button

Copy at 100%.

Grainline

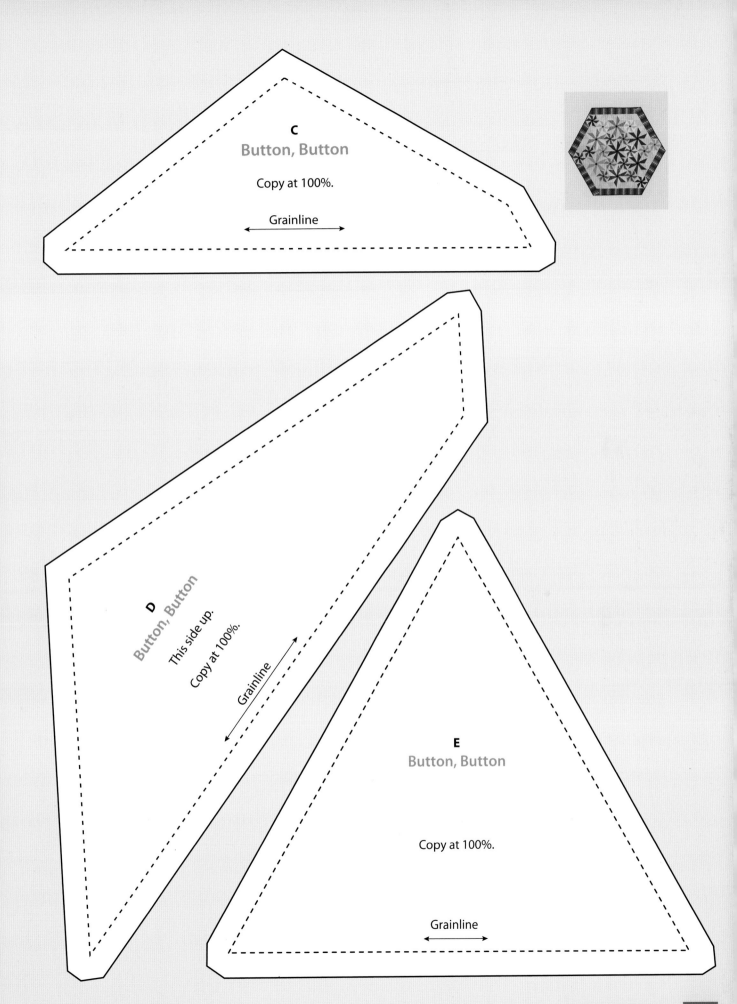

C
Button, Button

Copy at 100%.

Grainline

D
Button, Button

This side up.

Copy at 100%.

Grainline

E
Button, Button

Copy at 100%.

Grainline

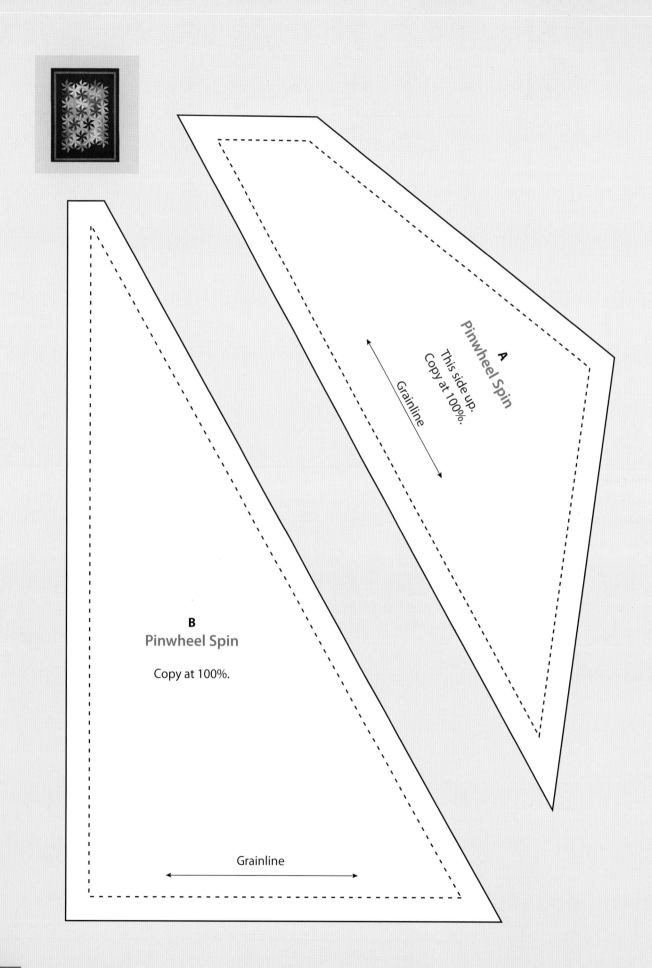

A

Pinwheel Spin

This side up.
Copy at 100%.

Grainline

B
Pinwheel Spin

Copy at 100%.

Grainline

Barbara Cline started creating quilts in her teens. Since then, she has had more than 30 years of experience teaching quiltmaking classes at a local sewing shop and creating beautiful quilts and patterns. Barbara worked at The Clothes Line fabric shop (now called Patchwork Plus) from fifth grade until she married and had children. She became a stay-at-home mother who pieced quilt tops to sell when she had time. When her youngest child entered kindergarten, she started working part-time at The Clothes Line again.

Barbara currently teaches classes at Patchwork Plus and loves to design and piece wallhangings and quilts from her home in Shenandoah Valley, Virginia. Her quilts have been shown and have won ribbons in various quilt shows and contests.

Barbara comes from a close-knit Mennonite family of quilters; her grandmother Vera Heatwole taught her daughters, granddaughters, great-great-granddaughters, and daughters-in-law to quilt. Every year the women gather for a sewing retreat, where they quilt, sew, and follow other creative pursuits. The family members and their quilts were featured in the Virginia Quilt Museum exhibition "Five Generations of Mennonite Quilts."

Previous book by Barbara Cline:

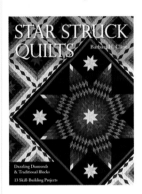

RESOURCES

Best Press spray starch
Mary Ellen Products, Inc.
www.maryellenproducts.com

Creative Grids 60° Triangle (8″ finished size) ruler
www.creativegridsusa.com

Pen-style Chaco Liner, flower-head pins
Clover: www.clover-usa.com

Perfect Piecer
Jinny Beyer: www.jinnybeyer.com

Retayne color fixative
G&K Craft Industries, Ltd.
www.gkcraft.com
(Also available from
www.dharmatrading.com.)

Shades SoftFuse
www.appliquedesigns.com/softFuse.htm

Note: Most of these and many other useful supplies and notions are also available at your local quilt shop.

Great Titles *from* C&T PUBLISHING

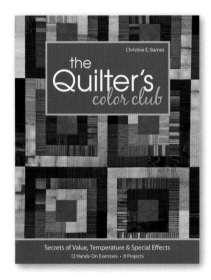

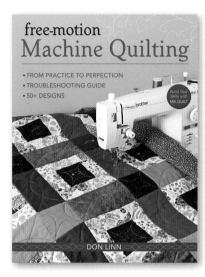

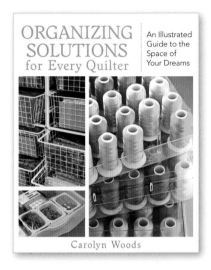

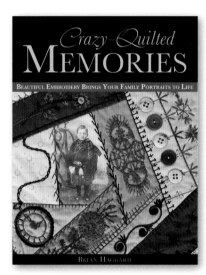

Available at your local retailer or **www.ctpub.com** *or* **800-284-1114**

For a list of other fine books from C&T Publishing, visit our website
to view our catalog online

C&T PUBLISHING, INC.

P.O. Box 1456
Lafayette, CA 94549
800-284-1114

Email: ctinfo@ctpub.com
Website: www.ctpub.com

C&T Publishing's professional photography services are now available to
the public. Visit us at www.ctmediaservices.com.

Tips and Techniques can be found at www.ctpub.com > Consumer
Resources > Quiltmaking Basics: Tips & Techniques for Quiltmaking & More

For quilting supplies:

COTTON PATCH

1025 Brown Ave.
Lafayette, CA 94549
Store: 925-284-1177
Mail order: 925-283-7883

Email: CottonPa@aol.com
Website: www.quiltusa.com

Note: Fabrics shown may not be currently available, as fabric
manufacturers keep most fabrics in print for only a short time.